Lessons From the Middle:
High-End Learning for Middle School Students

Lessons From the Middle:
High-End Learning for Middle School Students

Sandra Kaplan
Conceptual Development

Michael W. Cannon
Editor

Prufrock Press, Inc. • Waco, Texas

Elements of Depth and Complexity © Sandra Kaplan, Javits Grant Curriculum Project T.W.O.

Thinking Skills list, page 7: The work reported herein was supported under the Educational Research and Development Centers Program, PR/Award Number R206R950001-98, as administered by the Office of Educational Research and Improvement, U.S. Department of Education. The findings and opinions expressed in this report do not reflect the position or policies of the National Institute on the Education of At-Risk Students, the Office of Educational Research and Improvement, or the U.S. Department of Education. This document has been reproduced with the permission of the National Research Center on the Gifted and Talented.

PRUFROCK
PRESS INC.™

P.O. Box 8813
Waco, Texas 76714-8813
Phone: (800) 998-2208
Fax: (800) 240-0333
www.prufrock.com

CONTENTS

PREFACE

The mission statement of the Texas Association for the Gifted and Talented, "To promote awareness of the unique social, emotional, and intellectual needs of gifted and talented students and to impact the development of appropriate educational services to meet these needs," has been the guiding principle, not only of the general activities of the organization, but also of its publications. High school and elementary educational practices have been addressed in previous publications, and it was the decision of the TAGT Executive Board in 1999 that there was a need for a publication that focused on the middle school. This book was intended to present not only model lessons based on the core content areas (language arts, social studies, math, and science) and curriculum standards, but also a theoretical framework and directions for educators to prepare their own lessons according to this plan.

It was also decided that the book would be developed under the guidance of a nationally-recognized authority in the field of gifted education. Dr. Sandra Kaplan of the University of Southern California has been instrumental in the preparation of this book, from the initial planning and training of writers, to an intensive, ongoing commitment to editing and revising. Dr. Kaplan worked with the editor and team of writers to develop a lesson format that would guide teachers in utilizing depth and complexity with the standards in creating instructional experiences of real educational value to students. In addition, Dr. Kaplan wrote the Introduction, Differentiation Framework, Curriculum Design, and Open-Ended Lesson Plan sections that follow.

The writers who contributed lessons to this book are all outstanding educators who were selected based on their subject area expertise and experience in curriculum writing. Working with Dr. Kaplan and the editor, they worked tirelessly, writing, revising, and rewriting. Their model lessons set a high standard for middle school teachers.

The lessons have been grouped by grade level as they share a common theme. The grade level designations are, to some degree, for demonstration and example purposes only. In a particular classroom, lessons from other grade levels may be equally appropriate.

The curriculum standards used in the lessons are general in nature, rather than tied to a specific set of state or national standards. The following were consulted in the development of the curriculum standards: Standards for the English Language Arts (NCTE/IRA), National Science Education Standards (NRC), Principles and Standards for School Mathematics (NCTM), Curriculum Standards of Social Studies (NCSS), and the Texas Essential Knowledge and Skills (TEA).

The most important goal of this book is the hope that, with the examples of curriculum excellence and the theoretical background, teachers will begin to develop standards-based lessons and units of study that will promote high-end learning for gifted students in middle school.

ACKNOWLEDGMENTS

The development of this publication was sponsored by the Texas Association for the Gifted and Talented, a nonprofit organization of parents and professionals promoting appropriate education for gifted and talented students in the state of Texas. The following individuals contributed in the areas noted.

Dr. Sandra Kaplan, Conceptual Development

Sandra Kaplan is associate clinical professor for learning and instruction at the University of Southern California. She has served as the lead consultant for the Carnegie Middle Schools Project, Texas Education Agency, from 1993 to present. Dr. Kaplan is a past president of the National Association for Gifted Children (NAGC), of which she has been a member of since 1982. She is also a past president of the California Association for the Gifted. One of the world's foremost authorities in the field of gifted education, she has made presentations at the World Congress on Gifted, NAGC, and TAGT conferences. Recent honors include the Award of Achievement from the California Association for the Gifted and the Distinguished Service Award from NAGC.

Michael Cannon, Editor

Michael Cannon, publications editor for the Texas Association for the Gifted and Talented (TAGT), teaches in El Paso ISD. Active in gifted education for many years, he has been a member of the TAGT executive board since 1995. Named Outstanding Teacher of the Humanities in Texas in 1992, Cannon has published articles on gifted education in a number of state and national journals and books. In addition to presentations at regional, state, and national conferences, he also provides professional development and consults in the area of gifted education and curriculum development. He serves on the Development Committee, Statewide Gifted Performance Standards Project.

Kathie Schwartz, Language Arts Lessons

Kathie Schwartz, with 22 years experience teaching (13 in gifted education), currently teaches eighth grade Challenge Language Arts in Coppell ISD. She has written gifted curricula for the El Paso ISD middle school humanities program and the Cultural Arts Academy, for Putnam City School District in Oklahoma City, and the eighth grade gifted curriculum for Coppell ISD.

Mary Ann Clark, Social Studies Lessons

Mary Ann Clark, with 13 years experience in gifted programs, teaches Humanities, an integrated gifted program, at Hornedo Middle School, El Paso ISD. In addition, she has developed and presented professional development sessions in gifted education and has presented at local, state, and national middle school and gifted conferences. She has been recognized as Campus Teacher of the Year, TAGT Region XIX Outstanding Teacher of the Gifted, and Outstanding Teacher of the Humanities.

Wendy Coleman, Science Lessons

Wendy Coleman teaches gifted classes in the Fort Worth ISD. A middle school demonstration teacher with Dr. Sandra Kaplan, she has written gifted curricula for the Forth Worth ISD. In 1999 she was chosen Region XI Outstanding Teacher of the Gifted.

Shannon Peña, Math Lessons

Shannon McCreless Peña, Fort Worth ISD, has been a demonstration teacher for the Texas Carnegie Project and for the California Association for the Gifted. With Dr. Kaplan and a team of teachers, she helped develop a curriculum, "Think Like a Sociologist," which received an award from the National Association for the Gifted. Recently, she was selected as the Intel Chair for Teaching Excellence in Elementary Mathematics.

Leilani Calzada, Art Lessons

Leilani Tajiri Calzada, an art educator for 14 years, currently teaches art in Austin ISD. She previously taught art (including AP Art) at Burges High School in El Paso ISD for 12 years. She has written curricula for a middle school gifted program. Calzada holds degrees in art from the University of Texas at El Paso and in dance from Texas Women's University.

Janice Johnson, Instructional Consultant

Janice Johnson, with 16 years experience, currently teaches seventh grade science at Midway ISD and is the math, science, G/T facilitator for the district. She is regional director for the Science Teachers Association of Texas and a member of TAGT and the Association for Professional Educators. In 1999 Johnson was named the TAGT Regional Teacher of the Year.

INTRODUCTION

"There is insufficient time to differentiate the core curriculum for gifted students and still prepare these students to pass the state test at a high level of accomplishment."

This statement has been reiterated by teachers of the gifted throughout the nation. The teaching of a differentiated curriculum often is perceived as dichotomous from or in opposition to preparing students to attain curriculum standards at levels of success appropriate to the gifted. This is a false assumption.

The purpose of this publication is to illustrate to teachers of the gifted how they can be a successful teacher of the core or basic curriculum while simultaneously meeting the needs and expectations held for the performance of gifted students.

Perhaps the best way to resolve this artificial dilemma is to present it in a figurative form. The following diagram outlines the means by which *both* the core curriculum and differentiated curriculum can coexist and mutually reinforce each other.

The effective implementation of this goal is dependent on:

1. Defining the content, skill, or product elements of the curriculum standards that are appropriate and need to be emphasized for gifted students.

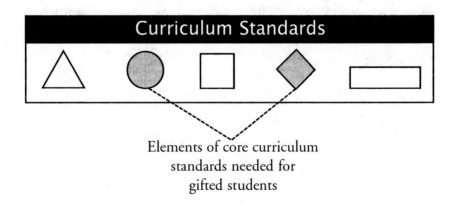

Elements of core curriculum
standards needed for
gifted students

The decision to identify certain elements is dependent on the evidence from an informal or formal assessment of student performance with the core curriculum standards. This performance provides data of prerequisite learning.

2. Emphasizing the elements of the curriculum standards necessitates the teacher's understanding of what appropriately constitutes differentiation or a differentiated curriculum.

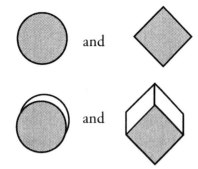 from the core curriculum are emphasized

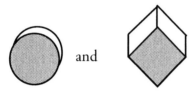 are differentiated to meet the needs of the gifted. Differentiating the core curriculum does not obliterate the core, but enhances the gifted students' potential to learn the material at a level commensurate to their needs and interests.

3. Differentiating the core curriculum for gifted students responds to their needs and still prepares them for a standardized test or any other form of assessment.

are part of a differentiated curriculum

These elements are part of the core curriculum even though

have been differentiated.

This diagram is offered as substantiation for the concept that the teaching of the core and differentiated curriculum can reinforce the attainment of curriculum standards while providing for the needs of gifted students.

DIFFERENTIATION FRAMEWORK

The concept of differentiation has been defined with an understanding of:
1. the contemporary theories describing differentiation; and
2. the diverse needs of gifted students.

Following is a delineation of the principles of differentiation that govern the design of the lessons and respond to the needs, abilities, and interests of gifted students:

Skills:

1. **Development of critical and creative thinking and problem-solving skills:**
   - Identify characteristics and attributes
   - Discriminate similar and different
   - Categorize
   - Classify
   - Rank, prioritize, sequence
   - See relationship
   - Identify the pattern
   - Determine cause/effect
   - Make analogies
   - Summarize
   - Formulate questions
   - Think inductively
   - Think deductively
   - Differentiate real vs. make-believe
   - Determine relevancy
   - Judge with criteria
   - Identify ambiguity
   - Determine strength of an argument

(National Research Center for Gifted and Talented, University of Connecticut)

2. **Development of research, learning-to-learn, and study skills.** Research skills include the skills that facilitate accessing resources and extrapolating needed information:
   - use parts of a book;
   - use multiple and varied references: encyclopedias, journals, newspapers, dictionaries, and so forth;
   - take notes;
   - outline;
   - summarize;
   - conduct a research study: historical, experimental, correlational, descriptive;
   - prioritize information/data;
   - organize information/data using graphic organizer; and

   - draw conclusions.

Learning-to-learn and study skills include the skills needed to facilitate "good" study habits or develop the behaviors of an emergent scholar:
- schedule time;
- recognize the need for preparation (tools, materials, and so forth);
- organize materials;
- solve potential problems that inhibit success or achievement; and
- seek appropriate assistance.

3. **Development of skills of production and presentation.** Production and presentation skills enable students to work independently and industriously:
   - create a work plan and basic design to follow in order to develop the product;
   - recognize materials needed to execute the product;
   - appreciate the relationship among process (producing) and content (understanding) and skills (thinking), as well as the relationship between artistic execution and the transmission of understanding and thinking; and
   - develop abilities to share the product appropriately.

Content:

1. Development of complex and universal concepts supported by facts and used to inductively form and deductively prove generalizations.
2. Comprehension of content in **depth** and **complexity**.
3. Introduction of areas of study or disciplines that are not traditionally part of the regular courses of study.

Icons	Dimension	Key Questions
(lips icon)	Language of the disciplines	• What terms or words are specific to the work of the _____? (disciplinarian)
(flower icon)	Details	• What are its attributes? • What features characterize this? • What specific elements define this? • What distinguishes this from other things?
(pattern icon)	Patterns	• What are the recurring events? • What elements, events, and ideas are replaced over time? • What was the order of events? • How can we predict what will come next?

Icons	Dimension	Key Questions
	Trends	<ul><li>What ongoing factors have influenced this study?</li><li>What factors have contributed to this study?</li></ul>
	Unanswered questions	<ul><li>What is still not understood about this area/topic/study/discipline?</li><li>What is yet unknown about this area/topic/study/discipline?</li><li>In what ways is the information incomplete or lacking in explanation?</li></ul>
	Rules	<ul><li>How is this structured?</li><li>What are the stated and unstated causes related to the description or explanation of what we are studying?</li></ul>
	Ethics	<ul><li>What dilemmas or controversies are involved in this area/topic/study/discipline?</li><li>What elements can be identified that reflect bias, prejudice, discrimination?</li></ul>
	Big Ideas, Generalizations, Principles, and Theories	<ul><li>What overarching statement best describes what is being studied?</li><li>What general statement includes what is being studied?</li></ul>

Icons	Dimension	Key Questions
	Over time	• How are the ideas related among the past, present, and future? • How are these ideas related within or during a particular time period? • How has time affected the information? • How and why do things change or remain the same?
	Different points of view	• What are the opposing viewpoints? • How do different people and characters see this event or situation?
	Interdisciplinary connections	• What are the common elements among the topics from the different disciplines? • How does this idea relate to all of these topics across the disciplines? • How do each of these topics across the disciplines contribute meaning to this idea?

(Curriculum Project T.W.O., A Javits Federally Funded Project from U.S. Office of Education Research)

Product:

1. Reinforcement of basic products fundamental to the disciplines: write a report and so forth.
2. Introductions of authentic products that support the work of the disciplinarians or professionals in the field. Production and presentation skills are the skills that facilitate the students' abilities to summarize and transmit understanding and mastery in a product. The selection of a product must correlate and reinforce:
   • the **nature** and **scope** of the content and skills that have been learned and reflect the core curriculum standards and dimensions of differentiation included in the lesson;
   • **authentic work of scholars** or professionals in the area of study. For example, in a history study, it may be more appropriate to produce a timeline than create a collage. The random selection of a product to match an artistic, rather than disciplinary, need might render the product less effective as a demonstration of the students' achievement of the core curriculum standards; and
   • **interests** and **abilities** of the gifted student.

CURRICULUM DESIGN

I. Teacher Preparation

◆ Background

This section provides the teacher with a frame of reference to plan and build a rationale for the development and/or use of the lessons. Within this section are elements to be addressed individually that guide the direction and extent of the lesson.

• Curriculum Standards

Curriculum standards are the basis for all curricular decision making. As teachers prepare lessons related to the standards, the following questions are used to determine the sequence or order of the teaching/learning activities and the scope or extensions for the teacher/learning activities:

1. What evidence is available or can be collected to verify prerequisite learning of the students?
2. What aspect or portion of the core curriculum standard can be compacted or replaced in order to gain time to differentiate the core curriculum standards?
3. What dimensions of differentiation are most responsive to the core curriculum standards?
4. How does the teaching of this lesson reinforce the core curriculum standards while simultaneously providing for a differentiated curriculum to meet the needs of the gifted students?

I. Teacher Preparation
· Background
· Framework
II. Lesson Format
· Motivation
· Input
· Output
· Culmination
· Extensions
  – Independent Research
  – Interdisciplinary Studies
  – Classical Connection
· Study Starters
· Arts Connection
· Assessment

• Curriculum Standard Level

The lessons have been classified according to the author's perceptions of their difficulty for gifted students. In general, because the lessons reinforce the curriculum standards, the level of difficulty represents both the gifted student's prerequisite learning of the elements of the curriculum standards and their readiness for the differentiated learning experience. Each level requires specific understanding of the attributes of differentiation in conjunction with specific mastery or expertise of the curriculum standards.

Level of Lesson	Level of Prerequisite Learning of the Standards	Level of Readiness for Differentiated Curricular Activities
Introductory	Standard has been explained; mastery not necessary.	Need introduction to differentiation; depth, complexity, and thinking skills.
Developmental	Standard has been explained; mastery or expertise has been attained.	Practice needed on research skills and discussion techniques.
Extension	Mastery and expertise is attained; readiness for new but related learning is evident.	Able to incorporate new areas and skills into an independent study.

• Time Required

The suggested time frame identified for each lesson is based on the author's intent for the implementation of the lesson. In essence, each lesson is a series of embedded mini-lessons or one or more mini-unit of study. This design alters the time needed to execute all or any part of the lesson. Other factors that can affect the time needed for the implementation of all facets of the lesson is dependent on:

1. Nature of the gifted program or service offered to gifted students. For example, using the lessons with gifted students in a homogeneous vs. heterogeneous setting will affect the time allocated to teaching the lesson.

2. Type of grouping practices used in the classroom. For example, whole-group teaching or instruction will demand a different time frame than teaching the same facets of the lesson in small groups or assigning them to students to work/study independently.

3. Availability of resources and/or materials. For example, some of the lessons require extensive use of ancillary resources.

4. Experiences and motivation of gifted students. For example, gifted students who are familiar with the dimensions outlined as appropriately differentiated will require less readiness and motivation to participate in the lessons.

5. Teacher expertise. For example, teachers who consistently incorporate the dimensions defined for a differentiated curriculum into their curriculum will need less time to prepare and teach these lessons.

• Getting Ready

This area of the lesson provides the teacher with some ideas that facilitate the necessary preparation to teach the lessons. This section does not present an exhaustive list of ideas. It does present some useful tips for the teacher.

◆ Framework

This section outlines the major facets of the lesson. Importantly, each facet contributes to the entire lesson.

• Theme

The theme is recognized as an organizing element, a theoretical concept used by curriculum developers to unite focus and interface aspects of the lesson or unit of study. The themes selected for these lessons are universal concepts such as change, conflict, systems, relationships, and power. On a continuum of knowing, concepts can be identified as simple, complex, and universal; these concepts represent the most broad and sophisticated level of knowing.

Example: truck (simple) transportation (complex) systems (universal)

It is important to note that the essential differences among these concepts is the degree to which they generalize to many and varied disciplines and the amount of definition or detail needed to define the concepts. Universal concepts are inclusive of other concepts and general to other concepts and disciplines. These characteristics of universal concepts makes them ideal themes for lessons. They represent the referent for the content assimilation and skill mastery of the lessons.

• Generalizations

The generalization is called a "big idea" that expresses a relationship between concepts. Generalizations are statements that are generally true or applicable to more than one situation. Generalizations in these lessons facilitate inquiry. They serve as the stimulus for students to gather evidence that can support the meaning of the generalization. In the context of these lessons, the generalizations are related to the universal concept or theme.

The following diagram explains the relationships among the theme, generalization, and curriculum standards.

Theme: A universal concept that organizes or focuses the lesson.

Generalization: A statement about the universal concept of theme that applies to multiple situations and initiates inquiry into the curriculum standards.

Standards: The concepts and facts that support the generalization and/or clarify its meaning.

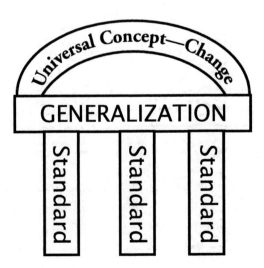

• Content Focus

The content focus is a brief description of the subject matter related to the core curriculum standards. It highlights the most critical features of the standards that are emphasized as subject matter in the lesson.

• Rationale

The rationale is an explanation of the value attributed to the study of the subject matter of the curriculum standards. The reason for including this element into the lesson is to provide teachers with a reference to use with students to establish the purpose and/or goal of the lesson. The rationale explains both the "why" and "so what" of studying the curriculum standards.

II. The Lesson Format

This section represents the actual presentation of the teaching process necessary to facilitate the students' understanding of content and mastery of skills supporting the curriculum standards and the dimensions of differentiation. Each lesson presents a comprehensive and sequential set of learning experiences or activities that facilitate the progression of the teaching/learning process. The development of the lesson is outlined for the teacher and written in a style that describes what the teacher is expected to do or the activities the teachers need to execute. It is imperative for teachers to understand that they can extend and augment the activities within the lesson in order to individualize the lesson, making it responsive to their particular class or students. However, teachers should recognize that the activities build on each other to develop a comprehensive and cumulative effect of learning; summarily omitting any part or activity could affect the outcome of the entire lesson. A certain fidelity to the proposed lesson is integral to its success and student achievement.

The design of the lessons is very basic. This format was selected to accommodate a wide range of teacher and student needs. The pattern of the lesson follows this outline:

Motivation	— stimulating the learner
Input	— providing background experiences to promote context understanding and skill mastery
Output	— providing experiences to practice learning through the development of written, illustrative, oral, and other products
Culmination	— synthesizing learning and giving the lesson closure
Extensions	— elaborating learning by providing opportunities to extended lessons

It is imperative for teachers to understand that lessons also could be written in formal models to teaching: Advance Organizer, Group Investigation, Direct Instruction (Six-Step Lesson Cycle), and so forth. Elements of these models have been informally incorporated into all the lessons.

◆ Motivation

The element of the lesson labeled motivation is designed to:
- stimulate interest in the focus area of study selected for the lesson;
- provide readiness for students to engage in the content and skills of the lesson;
- serve as an informal assessment of the students' prerequisite understanding of concepts and skill mastery; and
- provide for the personalization of the lesson to address the diversity among students.

In many lessons, the techniques or strategies used to motivate students include:
- questioning to evoke discovery and/or recall of previous knowledge;
- reading a literary selection to establish background knowledge;
- performing part of or an entire task to introduce the concept of skill; and
- completing a retrieval chart or some form of presenting and collecting information to initiate further study of the concepts and skills.

◆ Input

The element of the lesson labeled input refers to a collection of teaching/learning experiences that provide introduction or background for students to comprehend the concepts and master the skills of the lesson. This is the facet of the lesson that demands presenting the students with the subject matter. References, inquiry, or experiential activities, dialogue, discussions, and role-playing promote the students' orientation and/or foundation for the knowing and doing needed to further the teaching and learning of the curriculum standards and dimensions of differentiation outlined for the lesson.

◆ Output

The element of the lesson labeled output refers to a series of teaching and learning experiences that provide the practice needed to attain achievement of the core curriculum standards and dimensions of differentiation. Whereas the input facet of the lesson provides the introduction to content or skills, the output facet of the lesson provides the practice opportunities. These sections are symbiotically related and interdependent. They work together to reinforce the important principles of learning:
- accommodation and assimilation;
- introduction and practice; and
- setting expectations and attaining success.

◆ Culmination

The element of the lesson labeled culmination refers to the summary or synthesis of learning. It is in this facet of the lesson that students are expected to culminate their learning by creating an authentic product reflective of the comprehension of the concepts and mastery of the skills defined in the lesson. The product is perceived as an end or outcome of instruction and learning. Authentic products are those that can best transmit the students' learning and are most representative of the work produced by scholars in the area of study in which the students are working.

◆ Extensions

The element of the lesson labeled extension provides opportunities to elaborate and enrich the content or skill of the lesson. The concept of extension used here is not to be confused with the traditional concept of enrichment. Enrichment is sometimes perceived as a set of activities that are "rewards" offering gifted students experiences not typically afforded in the basic curriculum. Enrichment often is perceived by curriculum developers as a disjointed, incremental set of activities considered to be enticing to students, but lacking relevancy to the curriculum standards and differentiation. The following are the extensions of a lesson because they both reinforce the curriculum standards and the needs, interests, and abilities of gifted students:

- Independent research;
- Interdisciplinary studies;
- Classical connections;
- Study starters; and
- Arts connection.

• Independent Research

Independent research refers to the opportunity to enable a student to self-select an aspect of the content under study to pursue independently. The concept of the gifted student as researcher or investigator is referenced in the literature as an important learning experience because it affords them the time to:

- explore personal interest and abilities;
- develop unique interests;
- acquire study habits and self-regulatory skills; and
- practice independence of thought and behavior.

The steps of independent research are constant regardless of age or subject:

Independent Research

1. Select a topic.

2. Propose a set of study questions.

3. Gather data/information from multiple and varied references.

4. Organize the information.

5. Share the study.

Independent research necessitates the acquisition of research and study skills.

Basic Research Skills	Basic Study Skills
• Take notes • Paraphrase • Draw conclusions • Outline • Prioritize	• Define needed tools • Set time allocations • Determine learning style(s) and needs • Anticipate potential barriers

- **Interdisciplinary Studies**

Interdisciplinary studies refers to the inquiry of a universal concept and accompanying generalization using information across the disciplines. Defining, clarifying, exemplifying, and proving the generalization requires delving into the disciplines. Following is an example of the unit plan used to promote interdisciplinarity.

Universal Concept—Change

Generalization: Changes Lead to Change				
Discipline	Social Studies	Science	Math	Language Arts
Areas of Study	Ancient civilization		Geometry	
Facts to prove, clarify, and define the generalization	Changes in government lead to changes in political and philosophical beliefs		Changes in the number of line segments change its shape and name	

- **Classical Connection**

Classical connection refers to the introduction and subsequent inclusion of areas of study not traditionally considered to be part of the basic or core curriculum. The main purpose of this element is to provide students with opportunities to experience areas of study that promote new awareness, stimulate interests, arouse curiosity, and evoke dialogue and individual or group inquiry. Potential classic connections include:

Philosophy—an introduction to great thinkers and their beliefs such as Plato's *Republic*, Locke's belief that knowledge comes from the senses and that "all men are equal," and Spinoza's theory of relativitism.

Psychology—an exploration of how and why people behave as defined by Carl Jung and by Erikson's stages of man.

Fine arts—an introduction to the arts as a support to understanding the core content.

• Study Starters

The element of the lesson labeled study starters provides the teacher with open-ended worksheets that augment the learning of content and skills under study. Basically, the study starters initiate self-directed activities for students to further their comprehension and mastery of the core curriculum standards and dimensions of differentiation. The study starters are dependent on the teacher-directed sections of the lesson and cannot be used effectively without the demonstration and instruction of the teacher.

• Arts Connection

The element of the lesson labeled arts connection represents an opportunity for students to experience art paralleling some aspect of the content they are studying. Thorough directions are provided to the teacher and students to enable them to complete easily the artistic mini-project. Importantly, the arts connection is not intended to be implemented as an art lesson; rather, it is intended to be presented as an opportunity to demonstrate artistically understanding of the curriculum standards. In addition, neither the teacher nor the student need be artistically gifted to enjoy the artistic mini-project.

◆ Assessment

The element of the lesson labeled assessment describes the types of assessment a teacher can utilize in the classroom in order to measure the knowledge and skills students have derived from the teaching and learning processes.

- Formal ------------------------------ Informal
- Objective ---------------------------- Subjective
- Standardized ------------------------ Performance-based

These are the types of assessment techniques teachers can employ. However, the decision to choose one type of assessment technique over another is contingent on many classroom variables:

- nature and scope of what is to be assessed;
- purpose of the assessment;
- time allocated to assessment; and
- availability of evaluation instruments, and assessment tools.

The purpose for classroom assessments is to provide information about student progress or achievement relative to the content, skills, and product defined in the lesson; series of activities within a lesson; or lessons comprising a unit of study. Classroom assessment is the check for understanding (1) used by the teacher to measure achievement and plan curriculum and instruction and (2) used by the student to assess personal growth and establish self-efficacy as a gifted individual. Classroom assessment is a means to an end, rather than an end in itself. Stated more simply, classroom assessment is the assessment process that yields formative or in-progress information leading to a determination of the student's needs on the summative or "final" district and/or the state test.

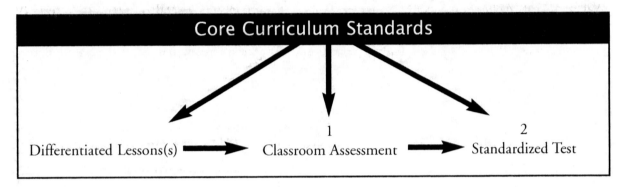

Rubrics represent a significant technique to assess the achievement of gifted students. While the rubric traditionally defines potential achievement at various levels from beginning to advanced, simple to sophisticated, novice to expert, it has been recognized by educators of the gifted that the "high end" of the rubric or the expert level is not only where gifted students should be performing, but where teachers should be identifying the curriculum and instruction for these students. The most pertinent question for teachers to answer is how to provide curriculum and instruction that reflects the level of "expert."

General Differentiated Curriculum Rubric

Novice	Acceptable	Expert
	(Note: Only the level of the rubric appropriate to the gifted has been articulated, and these have been written in general terms and need more specificity to be used for assessment purposes in the context of the classroom.)	• Given the content related to the curriculum standards, the gifted student will be able to use it as evidence to support an unusual concept and generalization. • Given content related to the curriculum standards, the gifted student can discuss how new information directly or indirectly reinforces the traditional content. • Given content related to the curriculum standards, the gifted student will use the dimension(s) of depth and/or complexity to study, discuss, and comprehend the content at more advanced and sophisticated levels. • Given content related to the curriculum standards, gifted students will select an aspect of the content to pursue as an independent study inclusive of: 1. a study plan; 2. a set of study questions; 3. collecting data from multiple and varied references; 4. applying appropriate learning skills; and 5. summarizing learning in an authentic, creative product to be shared. • Given basic skills relevant to the curriculum standards, gifted students will include and transcend the basic skills into the practice of critical thinking and problem solving. • Given a basic or traditional product, the gifted student will exemplify the content and skills of the curriculum standards, dimensions of depth and complexity, and universal theme in the product. • Given the study of the curriculum standards, the gifted student will be able to defend learning preferences, areas of interest, and describe traits to identify him- or herself as an emergent scholar.

The following rubric was developed by the writing team to give the teacher a guideline for assessing the level of student attainment in content/skills, products, and scholarship. This can be adapted to lessons in any content area.

	Acceptable	Recognized	Exemplary
Content/Skills	Describes, defines, applies skills to content.	Compare and contrast content and/or thinking.	Relates for a purpose existing knowledge and skills to new knowledge and skills between, among, and across disciplines.
Product	Summarizes knowledge in context of work—presentation (written, oral, graphic) or performance.	Distinguished from other products by greater emphasis placed on one or more attributes related to work.	Includes traits of sophisticated and accomplished work in the discipline. Exemplifies aspects of personal and professional risk taking.
Scholarship and Habits of Learning	Understands and uses abilities to perform task according to basic expectations.	Performs task independently to some degree.	Assumes responsibility for own abilities, knowing when and how to be independent.

OPEN-ENDED LESSON PLAN

This lesson format correlates with the lesson plans in this publication. The purpose of the open-ended lesson plan is to provide a guide to teachers in their development of lessons to teach the curriculum standards. Teachers often mention that one reason they are unable to meet the needs of the gifted in their classrooms is that they need a model that directs their curriculum planning and instruction. This model has been provided to meet the request of the many teachers who have expressed this need.

Since curriculum development is a decision-making process, the open-ended lesson plan model outlines the many and varied decisions teachers can make in order to differentiate curriculum and instruction of the curriculum standards. Following are the decisions teachers can make to develop differentiated lessons:

Objective: Use the template at the top of the page to articulate the objective. Remember that the objective reinforces the teaching of the curriculum standards.

Motivation: Select one of the options for motivating the students. Some of the options are more suited to motivating learning with respect to some disciplines. Make a good match between the type of motivation and the nature of the area to be studied.

Input: Select one of the proposed alternative modes to provide input to students. While each of these alternatives will work, select the alternative that best answers this question: How can the students most effectively be directed to inquire into this body of knowledge?

Output: Decide on the form of activity that would enable students to synthesize their understanding and display their mastery of what has been learned.

Culmination: Select a product that allows students to demonstrate or exhibit their learning in a concrete form and also enables them to have an experience that is a means to transmit the quality of their learning and provides them with an experience that stimulates their creativity and teaches them the art of productivity.

Extension: Choose one or more of the opportunities to allow students to engage in learning disciplines or areas of interest that are outside the parameters of the basic or core curriculum.

Assessment: Select the most expedient yet reliable means by which students can receive feedback about the quality of their learning and teachers can check understanding of the students' learning.

Open-Ended Lesson Plan

Objective Students will [thinking skill] [depth or complexity prompt] of

[content.] They will [resources and/or research skill] and create [product.]

Motivation

❏ Present a puzzlement or
a picture, literary passage,
artifact related to the area
of study.

❏ Initiate a discussion to
evoke interest in the
area of study.

❏ Dramatize an issue about the
area of study.

❏ Relate the area of study to
a current news article, report.

Input

❏ Introduce the advance
organizer in the form of a
set of content-based
questions or statements to
initiate exploration of the
content under study.

❏ Introduce a selected set of
dimensions of **depth/complexity**
to guide inquiry of the content.
For example, students will
identify patterns and trends
in the study of [   ] .

❑ Define the references to be used to investigate a universal concept such as **change** or **conflict** using the content under study.

❑ State the generalization for students to prove or exemplify with the content.

Output

❑ Create a class or group retrieval chart.

❑ Provide open-ended worksheets.

❑ Outline a task to perform to conceptualize and synthesize the learning.

Culmination

❑ Provide students with an authentic product that demonstrates understanding of content and mastery of skills.

Extensions

❑ Allow students to self-select an aspect of the content to investigate as independent research.

❑ Extend the skills learned to one or more other disciplines.

❑ Relate all learning to the theme or universal concept [   ].

❑ Introduce a new discipline, relate to the content. Consider philosophy, psychology, and so forth.

❑ Provide an art experience.

Assessment

❑ Provide informal assessment by "checking for understanding" using questions, prompts for discussion, and so forth.

❑ Discuss qualities of learning using a rubric developed for the lessons and/or product.

❑ Prepare teacher-made traditional and perform-ance-based test items.

❑ Engage students in discussions and journal writing to discern group and personal evaluation of the lesson.

❑ Conduct a personal (teacher) evaluation of how the lesson was taught.

Sixth GRADE

Theme: Conflict

- Language Arts—Epics and Ballads
- Social Studies—Religion and Political Change
- Math—Probability & Statistics: Collecting Data
- Science—It's in the Genes!

Epics and Ballads
They Don't Make Heroes Like They Used to— Or Do They?

I. Teacher Preparation

◆ **Background**
Time Required: 5–10 class periods

Getting Ready
For this lesson you will need the following:
- sample ballads such as *Barbara Allan*, *Lord Randall*, and *Casey at the Bat*;
- excerpts from epics including *Gilgamesh*, *Beowulf*, and *Song of Roland*;
- copies of recent obituaries; and
- contemporary visual art and music that demonstrates conflict and/or tells a story.

Curriculum Standards

The student will:

Primary Standard
- Recognize how features of a genre build understanding of the human experience.

Embedded Content and Skills
- Use effective rate, volume, pitch, and tone for the audience and setting.
- Read for varied purposes such as to be informed, to be entertained, to appreciate the writer's craft, and to discover models for his or her own writing.
- Interpret text ideas through such varied means as journal writing, discussion, enactment, and media.
- Connect, compare, and contrast ideas, themes, and issues across a text.
- Capitalize and punctuate correctly to clarify and enhance meaning.

Curriculum Standard Level:
Introductory X   Developmental   Extension

◆ Framework

Theme: Conflict

Generalization: Varying relationships (direct, indirect, natural, imposed) are catalysts in creating varying types of conflicts (friendly or adversarial, negative or positive).

Content Focus: Narrative poetry/epics and ballads—students will read classic epics and ballads in order to be able to identify key features and to use this as a springboard in writing their own modern epic or ballad.

Rationale: The study of narrative poems, especially epics and ballads, is important in understanding other cultures and the heritage that has been passed down to us as a result of their oral traditions. These epics and ballads help us understand the values and beliefs of other societies and help us see parallels of human behavior, values, or conflicts across cultures and time. The study also reminds us of the importance of storytelling in our daily lives.

Differentiation Framework

Thinking Skills	Depth/Complexity	Research	Products
• Note ambiguity • Determine cause/effect	• Pattern • Trends • Point of view	• Original documents • Authorship/origin	• Write an original epic or ballad

Thinking Skills

- **Note ambiguity**—to sense inconsistencies, gaps, and incongruities.
  Example: Students will note the ambiguity in determining character motivation, as well as the author's purpose in writing as a reflection of societal values.
  Example: Students will note the ambiguity in defining the type of relationships between and among characters and the conflict that results from these relationships.
- **Determine cause/effect**—to explain why certain events occurs and the results of this action, activity, and events.
  Example: Students will determine the causes of a hero's actions and the direct and indirect effects of these actions on character development, plot structure, and conflict resolution.

Depth/Complexity

- **Pattern**—repetitive action; repetitive activities.
  Example: Students will identify the patterns that distinguish an epic or ballad within or across cultures.
  Example: Students will identify the patterns of conflict that motivate the actions of characters and define the cultural values presented in the ballad or epic.

- **Trends**—the external social, economic, political, and cultural forces that shape actions and events.
  Example: Students will identify the values and trends of a society or culture based on the traits the hero depicts or embodies.
- **Point of view**—the effect of roles, time, place, or perceptions of events and/or actions.
  Example: Students will describe and judge the perceptions of the character from the vantage points of author, reader, and critic.

Research

- **Original documents**—Primary documents.
  Example: Students will compare a document of the epic's or ballad's culture and time in order to define the type and style of language from that type of writing to that used in the epic or ballad being studied.
- **Authorship/Origin**—the significance of literary sources.
  Example: Students will use primary references such as the oldest versions of the epics or ballads studied, especially in the original language of the literary piece, as a source for comparing authorship.

Product

- **Write a 21st century epic or ballad.**
  Example: Students will be given the basic elements (setting, hero, and so forth) of an epic or ballad to incorporate into the patterns of their own epic or ballad. Students will be expected to use these benchmarks to guide the development of their own poem: creativity, accuracy of form, conventions of quality writing, and utilization of the writing process (specifically, edit and revise). Students will be able to explain verbally the source and pattern of the epic or ballad created.

II. The Lesson

◆ Motivation

1. Chart why and how people have communicated in written, oral, and graphic forms over the years.

How We Communicate		
Written	**Oral**	**Graphics**
Stories Letters Documents	Oral History Radio Music	Hieroglyphics Pictures Charts Advertisements

2. Examine the similarities and differences between these forms of communication. Create a web or chart to facilitate discussion.

3. Ask students to respond to the question: How do the purposes for communicating affect the form of communication? Consider purposes of communication such as to entertain, inform, teach, sell, and so forth.

4. Discuss the "modern" form of rap or other form of modern music as compared to older forms of communication such as oral history or storytelling. Introduce a written set of rap lyrics ("Changes" by Tupac Shakur; "Paul Revere" by Beastie Boys; "Tricky" by RUN-DMC are possibilities. Be sure to preview the songs you choose before playing them, as many have potentially offensive lyrics). Ask students to read the lyrics to determine the degree to which they believe the rap version contains the traditional elements of a story: setting, character, plot (introduction, complication, rising action, climax, falling action, denouement), point of view, conflict, mood, theme, and so forth. Ask the students to set this up in chart form.

5. Give students the lyrics to a ballad. Identify the traditional story elements that are found within a ballad and the specific features that distinguish the story as a ballad. Have students set up a graphic organizer with the following headings:
   - Common or Traditional Story Elements; or
   - Specific Elements Particular to a Ballad.

Teacher Notes

Locate copies of a ballad and an excerpt from an epic. There are two types of epics and ballads. The folk epic and folk ballad were a part of the oral tradition of a nation. The literary epic and literary ballad were written based on the original style.

Ballads

Traits

- Song-like poem that tells a story that often ends in surprise.
- Emotionally charged/intriguing atmosphere
- Language is simple.
- Repetition of words or phrases is used (often includes a refrain).
- Themes are universal, such as love, death or murder, feuds, revenge, or jealousy (topics of today's tabloids and soap operas).
- Stories often revolve around historical events such as shipwrecks, battles, and disasters.
- Written in four-line stanzas.
- Have pattern of rhyme (abcb) and rhythm— usually written in iambic meter (one unaccented syllable followed by an accented syllable; e.g. "be - cause").

Titles

Traditional: *Robin Hood and the Monk, Hugh of Lincoln, Willie O' Winsbury, The Highwayman, Lord Randall, Barbara Allan, Bonnie George Campbell,* The *Wreck of the Hesperus, Yankee Doodle, Lochinvar, Get Up and Bar the Door, The Ballad of William Sycamore.*

American ballads: *Casey Jones, John Henry,* and *Casey at the Bat.* (Including one of the American ballads will allow students to see how the pattern remained even across cultures and time.)

6. Ask students to rap the ballad. Discuss how rap enhances or facilitates comprehension of the ballad and why the ballad is so easily adaptable to rap. (Note: It would be interesting to determine what other genres are adaptable to rap and why this adaptability exists for some genres and not for others.)

◆ Input

Discovery Process

1. Discuss the societal value of discovery and tell students that today they are going to assume the role of explorers. Provide an example that helps students recognize that explorers often have ambiguous information that they have to decipher in order to find the important details that lead to discovery. (You might discuss information that Columbus had when he prepared to sail "around the world.") Inform students that they will employ the behaviors and attitudes of an explorer to decipher the ambiguous features of ballads and epics.

2. Discuss the concept of features. Have students look at a portrait of a face and discuss the features (eyes, eyebrows, nose, mouth, cheeks, and so forth) that distinguish one portrait from another. Discuss how facial features distinguish us from other individuals and often from other cultural groups. Relate the concept of distinguishing features to architecture (a Gothic cathedral to a Frank Lloyd Wright structure or to the Taj Majal or to St. Basil's Cathedral in Moscow) or art styles (Leonardo da Vinci's *Mona Lisa* to a Picasso or Andy Warhol portrait). Parallel the concept of features to the traits of a genre they have studied previously (mystery, short story, novel).

3. Divide students into small groups.
   - Instruct the students to read the poems and then hypothesize the features (traits) of a ballad and an epic.
   - Give each group two sheets of butcher paper or other large sheets of paper on which to record the features.
   - Distribute one copy of a ballad and an excerpt from an epic to each group.
   - Hang the charts from the various groups around the room and have the students summarize and categorize the features the groups have listed in order to create "final" class definitions of the specific features of an epic and a ballad.
   - Compare the features that distinguish a ballad from an epic.
   - Have students look up *ballad* and *epic* in a reference book to authenticate their definitions and then refine them as needed.

4. Review the concept of theme as it is used in literature. Relate the use of theme in literature to the same themes used across the curriculum: "the threads that tie together meaning"; "an organizer for information, thoughts."
   - Discuss conflict as a literary *and* curricular theme. For example, conflict as a literary theme especially depicts the essence of characters' interactions with each other and perpetuates the plot; conflict as a curricular theme is the focal point of study across topics and/or disciplines.
   - Discuss the role of conflict in the ballad read for the rap. Ask students to provide examples of the theme of conflict in social studies, science, math, and so forth.

5. Define a generalization as a statement that bridges two or more concepts or ideas. For example, a literary generalization is "all literature reveals the inner thoughts or values of the author."

- Ask which two concepts are being connected or bridged (literature and author's thoughts or values).
- Introduce the generalization related to conflict: varying relationships create varying forms of conflict.
- Ask students to define the ideas or concepts bridged in this generalization.
- Define varying forms of relationships (direct, indirect, natural, imposed) and conflict (friendly/adversarial, negative/positive).
- Instruct students to prove or disprove the generalization using the information from the ballad (or epic) previously read. Discuss this activity as a form of deductive reasoning.

6. Provide students with other ballads and/or epics.

- Ask students to determine if their perceptions of conflict in a single ballad or epic generalizes across the two genres.
- Pose the question: Why is the theme (conflict) and related generalization (conflict is a consequence of varying relationships or varying relationships result in varying forms of conflict) relevant to all ballads and epics?

Teacher Notes

Epics

Traits

- Long, narrative poem told in elevated language (formal style).
- Setting may be a nation, the earth, or the universe.
- Hero with superhuman abilities or spiritual powers who has, however, a human weakness. (The hero may be a commoner or noble and often has an unusual birth or childhood. He might be raised by foster parents, and he might discover his real identity later.)
- Heroic deeds generate national or cultural pride.
- Hero embodies traits valued in that society (e.g., wisdom, courage, hospitality).
- Quest of hero, with difficulties and conflict, is central. The hero must often enter another world or the underworld to accomplish the task.
- Supernatural forces or mythological characters. These forces or characters often help the hero.
- Characters are often stereotypical.
- Theme (often stated at the beginning) is important to that culture or nation.
- Story begins in medias res (in the middle of the action).

Titles

- Be sure that the excerpt of the epic includes enough of the original that students can "discover" the features of an epic without being weighed down with the whole literary piece. Many literature books include good excerpts from epics such as *Gilgamesh*, *Beowulf*, *The Iliad*, *The Odyssey*, *Aeneid*, *Song of Roland*, *Poem of El Cid*, and *Mahabharata*.

◆ Output

1. Introduce the concepts of trends and patterns. Use the newspaper as a reference to review the effects of trends on "news." Discuss patterns of reporting news and the patterns inherent in news events (history repeats itself).

Teacher Notes

You will want to find interesting obituaries on contemporary individuals, preferably someone who has made a mark on the world in some way. *Time* and *Newsweek* magazines have obituaries. Be sure to use obituaries that have ample information about the deceased.

2. Discuss the use of trends and patterns in conducting a comparative literary analysis—when it is conducted, how it is conducted, and why it is useful.

3. Introduce the following documents to small groups of students:
   - the front page of a recent newspaper (especially one that depicts trends in current issues and patterns of society);
   - modern obituaries;
   - 20th-century art; and
   - musical selection.

4. Ask students to review the documents to conduct a comparative analysis of the trends and patterns inherent within and across the documents. Consider the key trend of conflict in its many forms. Ask students to set up the chart below as a graphic organizer.

Type of Document	Trends	Patterns

◆ Culmination

1. Use the Study Starter to brainstorm words and phrases derived from their interpretation of the above documents. Include these words in the outline of the features of a ballad or epic.

2. Have students work individually or in small groups to create a ballad or epic based on modern conflicts identified in current trends and patterns.

3. Tell students they will become traveling minstrels and share their epics or ballads with other classes *or* produce a video of their modern epic or ballad to share with the class or other classes. This could include props and backdrops, as well as music that would reflect the attributes of the ballad or epic being recited/performed.

◆ Extensions
—Independent Research Topics
- **Independent Research—Legends**
1. Introduce the relationship between the narrative prose of legends and that of ballads and epics. Identify similarities and differences between the genres.

2. Provide a list of legends from which students could select for further study:
   - Folk legends—Robin Hood, Pecos Bill, Johnny Appleseed, John Henry, Paul Bunyan, and Blarney Stone.
   - Native American legends—Hiawatha
   - Modern legends—Isadora Duncan, Winston Churchill, Babe Ruth, Princess Diana, John F. Kennedy, Marilyn Monroe, James Dean, and Martin Luther King, Jr.
   - Family legends—stories that have been repeated within the student's family (oral tradition) and handed down from one generation to another.

3. Define comparative literary analysis as the basis of the independent study:
   - Describe the features of the legend that distinguish it from ballads and epics.
   - Describe the trends and patterns within the legend.
   - Describe the role of conflict in the legend.

Teacher Notes

Newspaper—Students will easily pick out the key features of the front page of a newspaper.

Obituary—They will struggle a little more with the features of an obituary, so help them see the difficulties (conflicts) this person dealt with in life. War? Great Depression? Deaths of family members? Overcoming poverty? What heroic qualities did the person demonstrate and how did he or she embody values of the society—loyalty, perseverance, hospitality, entrepreneurial skills? Did he or she accomplish something against tremendous odds?

Art—Select a contemporary piece of art that has an element of conflict or tells a story—paintings, magazine ads, book illustrations, music videos (MTV), or any other type of art. Prints and slides are available from the Smithsonian's National Gallery of Art, as well as from local art museums.

Music—Choose a selection that evokes the idea of conflict, such as the theme from *Jaws*, *Star Wars*, or another movie. Students already have a familiarity with music as a form of communication. Have students think about cartoons or movies such as *Jaws*. Ask them how can they tell when conflict is building just by listening to the music. Note how the musical selection changes and discuss these changes and what they might imply.

- **Additional options:**
1. Write a journal told from the point of view of the main character of the legend, write and perform a play based on the legend, or create a pop-up book that retells the story for an elementary student.
2. Some modern writers classify George Lucas' *Star Wars* series and J.R.R. Tolkien's trilogy, *The Lord of the Rings* trilogy, as epics. Have students do an analysis of them to see if these selections fit the pattern as defined.

—Interdisciplinary Options
- **History/Social Studies**
1. Research the country or society representing an epic in order to discover:
   - the historical basis of the people, places, and events of the epic; and
   - whether the societal values reflected in the epic are still important to that country or society today.
2. Discuss other forms of storytelling such as cave paintings and art found at ancient burial sites in the country or region from which the epic originated.

- **Visual/Performing Arts**
1. Instruct students to find art, music, plays, poems, operas, and so forth that are based on the characters or events of an epic, ballad, or legend. Example: The Arthurian legend inspired poems such as "The Lady of Shalott," "The Faerie Queen," and "Tristram and Iseult"; movies such as *The Sword in the Stone, Camelot, Excalibur,* and *Monty Python and the Holy Grail*; books such as *Le Morte D'Arthur, The Mists of Avalon, The Return of Merlin,* and *The Once and Future King*; and operas such as *Lohengrin, Parsifal,* and *Tristram and Isolde,* as well as numerous paintings and short stories.
2. Define montage (art that is a combination of elements from separate sources. It can be a combination of pictures, objects, or designs. In film, it can be a mixture of shots that depict a passage of time or provides a great deal of information in a short period of time). Instruct students to create a montage of poetry readings, movie/opera clips, works of art, and so forth set to appropriate music representing the theme of conflict that connects all of these pieces.

—Classical Connections
1. The "Ologies"
   - Review the "ologies" as particular studies or bodies of information:
     —Biology
     —Zoology
     —Anthropology
     —Psychology
     —Sociology
   - Introduce the work of a sociologist as one who studies group dynamics and the interactions among people in groups and institutions. Present a sociogram to students illustrating the concept of patterns of interaction among people. Discuss why some individuals are euphemistically titled "sheep" while others are called "lion kings" in a group. Apply the understanding of group interactions and dynamics to the relationships among characters in a ballad or epic. Determine "leaders" or lion kings from "followers" or sheep and how such roles occur and are important in the characters of a story.
2. Philosophy
   Courage was an important quality of heroes in epics. In Plato's dialogue *Laches,* courage is discussed as Socrates asks for definitions of the term and probes the understanding of those present. Read the dialogue with students or summarize it for them. Conduct a discussion about what constitutes courage (or friendship, or honor, or faithfulness, or other

qualities of characters in epics or ballads). The class or small groups may define, find examples, and make connections with current events or their own life.

◆ **Assessment/Evaluation**

Create a rubric for student self-assessment. Use these descriptors to form the levels of the rubric:

1. their ability to define and distinguish the traits of a ballad and epic and following these conventions in their own modern versions;
2. sophistication of style (poetic language, strong vocabulary choice, etc.);
3. language usage including spelling, punctuation, grammar (editing and revising);
4. ability to think and work independently; and
5. creativity (risk taking).

—Adaptations for Other Grade Levels

Elementary—Fables, fairy tales, and tall tales could be used to study genres that tie to the oral tradition. These also work well with the study of conflict in narratives. Secondary—use an entire epic instead of an excerpt. Use archetypes in analysis.

Contemporary Courage or True Love Never Dies

Write A Modern Epic Using Current Events/Characters

In writing your epic, follow the conventions of this type of narrative. To help you write your epic, use two or more of the following sources: the front page of a newspaper, a recent obituary, a 20th-century piece of art, and/or a modern musical selection. You may use those given to you by your teacher or you may find your own. Give your epic a title. Use the following as the basis for your epic:

- **Universal theme** (must be appropriate to this nation and time period)
- **Setting**
  — Time
  — Place
- **Character**
  — Protagonist
      Special powers
      Character traits that represent the time
  — Antagonist
      Character traits
  — Supernatural/mythological characters
  — Stereotyped characters (What stereotypical characters will you use?)
- **Plot**
  — Hero's quest
  — Conflict
  — Rising action (list the major events)
  — Climax
  — Resolution/Denouement

Evaluation/Assessment

Grading will be based on these factors:

- ❏ Following the genre conventions, including how they reflect societal values

- ❏ Sophistication of style (poetic language, strong vocabulary choice, etc.)

- ❏ Language usage, including spelling, punctuation, grammar (editing and revising)

- ❏ Ability to think and work independently

- ❏ Creativity/risk taking

Contemporary Courage or True Love Never Dies

Create A Modern Ballad
Based on Current Events/People

The narrative poem should be written in simple language, but with depth of emotion/intrigue and including rhythm and rhyme. It should have a title and at least six stanzas. To help you create your ballad, use the front page of a newspaper, a recent obituary, a 20th-century piece of art, and/or a modern musical selection given to you by your teacher or that you find your own. Use the following as a basis for your ballad:

- **Universal theme** (love, death, revenge, jealousy)
- **Setting**
  — Time
  — Place
- **Characters**
  — Protagonist
  — Antagonist
  — Secondary Characters
- **Plot**
  — Conflict
  — Rising action (list the main events)
  — Climax
  — Resolution/Denouement
- **Refrain/repetition** of important words or phrases (List important words/phrases or a refrain that can be used.)
- **Music**—What music will you use if you sing it?

Evaluation/Assessment

Grading will be based on these factors:

❏ Following the genre conventions, including how they reflect societal values

❏ Sophistication of style (poetic language, strong vocabulary choice, etc.)

❏ Language usage, including spelling, punctuation, grammar (editing and revising)

❏ Ability to think and work independently

❏ Creativity/risk taking

Expressionistic Art

*Art is a powerful means of telling the stories of
great individuals and heroic deeds.*

Artists throughout the ages have been inspired by stories of the past. Some have chosen to illustrate myths through paintings, printmaking, sculptures, and drawings, while others have chosen to use these art forms to recreate moments in history. These personal expressions of historical accounts are unique inventions that give the viewer an opportunity to experience the stories from a visual perspective full of emotion and narrative expression.

A powerful example of this expressionistic style of art is the sculpture the *Burghers of Calais* by the artist Auguste Rodin. It pays tribute to seven heroic citizens of the town of Calais who gave their lives to the English during the Hundred Years' War to spare the lives of their fellow citizens. Each of the seven individuals portrayed in the sculpture expresses emotions as unique as the individual. Rodin shows their despair, sense of loss, anguish, and surrender. This life-size sculpture was cast in bronze so that the viewer could experience the very real presence of the heroes.

One of the castings can be seen in Washington D.C. at the Hirshhorn Museum and Sculpture Garden at the Smithsonian Institution.

Objective

The students will explore the sculpture of the *Burghers of Calais* by Auguste Rodin. The students will develop appreciation through four steps of art criticism: description, analysis, interpretation, and judgment.

Materials
- art history books
- posters or other pictures of the sculpture
- ruled paper for writing
- pencil or pen
- measuring tape

Procedure
1. The first step of art criticism is **description**. What do you see? This step requires the student to study carefully the sculpture and list all the things the student sees. One item on the list should be seven figures of men. The next item might reflect upon the attire of the men. How are the men positioned? Is the sculpture made of wood, stone, or metal? An important source for finding this information is the credit line of the work of art. The credit line will list the medium and the dimensions of the work. It is important to consider the dimensions of the work because a reproduction of a work of art will seldom be the exact size of the actual work. In the case of the *Burghers of Calais,* realizing the actual dimensions (91" x 96½" x 30") will give the students a different perception of Rodin's masterpiece. Pull out the tape measure and show the class the dimensions. The dimensions are always listed in the order of height, width, and depth.

2. The next step requires the student to make **observations** of the work regarding its organization. How did the artist organize the work? Notice the elements of art and how the artist used them. The elements are color, space, line, shape, texture, value, and form. With regard to Rodin's sculpture, the students will notice the texture, color, and size. Students will notice how the artist exaggerated the sizes of parts of the figures to communicate the weight of their sacrifice and sorrow.

3. **Interpretation** is the step that gives the students an opportunity to speculate about the artist's intentions. What is the artist trying to tell us? In the case of Rodin's sculpture, one might imagine what the sculpture is about. Without the aid of the history of the work, this can be the most challenging step in art criticism. Each student will develop an interpretation. Each of these unique interpretations is valid. Encourage the students to be thoughtful about their interpretations. Once again, they should write their interpretations on paper. Ask for volunteers to share their conclusions with the class.

4. Finally the students will have an opportunity to be the critics. The **judgment** step questions the success of the artwork. The student must be honest in making the judgment about the artwork. The judgment should be qualified. Each student's opinion is valid if the student can qualify his or her opinion. The purpose of these steps in art criticism is to explore art works through a thoughtful process designed to qualify the relevance of a work of art to an individual. The more often a student engages in this exploration, the more appreciative he or she will be of art.

Evaluation

Did the students participate in the lesson? Did the students gain an appreciation for Auguste Rodin's *Burghers of Calais*?

Art Reference Books

The art book (1998). London: Phaidon.

Janson, H. W. (1997). *The history of art*. New York: H. Abrams.

Strickland, C. & Boswell, J. (1992). *The annotated Mona Lisa: A crash course in art history from prehistoric to postmodern*. Kansas City: Andrews & McNeel.

Tansey, R. (1995). *Gardner's art through the ages*. New York: HBJ.

Religion and Political Change

I. Teacher Preparation

◆ **Background**
Time Required: 2 weeks

Getting Ready
For this lesson you will need the following:
- set of character cards; and
- art supplies, including heavy duty foil, string, and india ink.

Curriculum Standards

The student will:

Primary Standard
- Examine the role played by religious institutions in the lives of individuals and the impact of these institutions on the community.

Embedded Content and Skills
- Describe characteristics of selected contemporary societies that resulted from historical events.
- Explain the significance of individuals from selected societies past and present and their influence on selected historical and contemporary societies.
- Analyze similarities and differences among selected world societies and explain examples of conflict between and among cultures.
- Compare characteristics of institutions in selected contemporary societies.
- Explain aspects that link or separate cultures and societies.

Curriculum Standard Level:
Introductory   Developmental   **Extension X**

◆ Framework

Theme: Conflict

Generalization: Conflict can be covertly or overtly defined and exhibited. A variety of traditions, values, and beliefs from both within a religion and different religions may be linked to create positive political change through active (violent) or passive (nonviolent) conflict.

Content Focus:
- Through a melding of different religious and secular doctrines and traditions, Mohandas Gandhi was able to create large-scale political change through a largely nonviolent conflict.
- This lesson is taught once students have studied the five major world religions of Christianity, Islam, Hinduism, Buddhism, and Judaism. The teacher may need to give background information regarding Sikhism and Jainism.

Rationale: By defining, describing, and judging the role one individual played in bringing a nonviolent resolution to a conflict, students will be able to discover the relationship of religion, tradition, and philosophical ideas in creating change.

Differentiation Framework

Thinking Skills	Depth/Complexity	Research	Products
• Determine cause/effect • Make analogies • Determine strength of an argument	• Ethics • Big ideas • Different points of view	• Historical research using print and non-print references	• Panel discussion about religion and culture

Thinking Skills
- **Determine cause and effect**—to define the relationship between why things occur and the consequence of their occurrences.
  Example: Students will relate philosophical ideas to religious beliefs of a culture by providing examples and bibliographic situations.
- **Make analogies**—To use figurative language to describe different things.
  Example: Students will describe the comparison between different religions or philosophical ideas using metaphors.
- **Determine the strength of an argument**—to provide evidence for a citation to substantiate a position or point of view.
  Example: Students will authenticate a philosophical point of view such as free will and self-actualization using primary sources.

Depth/Complexity
- **Ethics**—what is valued in a culture.

Example: Students will identify socialization methods used by cultures to foster philosophical or religious beliefs.

- **Big ideas**—generalizations, principles, theories, and laws inherent in a body of knowledge. *Example:* Students will apply the theory (*People use religion as a foundation to form beliefs*) to the philosophical beliefs of a culture.
- **Points of view**—the particular perceptions of all individuals assuming a role or responsibilities. *Example:* Students will describe the conflicting points of view regarding the given philosophical ideas of a culture.

Research

- **Historical Research**—conduct a retrospective analysis of an area of study using multiple and varied references. *Example:* Students will form or select a question to investigate a historical topic.

Product

Students will take a stand to discuss the value or significance of religion to the identity of a culture and to its political organization.

II. The Lesson

◆ Motivation

1. Ask students to share a family tradition with the class. The tradition may be expressed in many different forms: a passage from a selection of literature, an object that is passed from generation to generation that is of special significance, a song or selection of music, a picture or portrait, a food of special significance, and so forth.
   Students are expected to answer these questions about the traditions they have shared:
   - How did it originate?
   - Why is it significant?
   - Who in the family is the archivist (keeper) of the tradition? Why?
2. Have students share their traditions with the class. Students should address the three questions identified for sharing a family traditions.
3. Following the presentations of family traditions, initiate a class discussion to respond to these questions:
   - What are the common traits or purposes shared by traditions?
   - What are the relationships between traditions and ethnicity?
   - What are the relationships between traditions and religion?
   - What are the roles between religion and culture?
   - What is the relationship between traditions and cultural borrowing?
   - When do traditions evoke conflict?
4. Develop a retrieval chart to summarize the student responses to the above questions using key ideas as prompts to synthesize ideas discussed by students.

Traditions	
Elements	**Key Ideas**
• Origin • Purpose • Reflection of religion • Reflection of culture	

- Use the retrieval chart to generalize the information about traditions to these questions:
  — Which traditions reflect the culture of our community, state, or nation?
  — How do traditions reflect belief systems?
  — Why do some definitions reflect conflict experienced by cultures?

◆ **Input**

1. Have students make and complete a chart of the five major world religions as a review. Students could complete the chart in several types of working groups:
   - each group responsible for a particular religion; or
   - each group assigned a specific aspect such as a "founder" across the major religions; or
   - either homogeneous ability/interest groups or heterogeneous cooperative groups.

2. Review orally the information found on the chart once all groups have completed it. As the charts are reviewed, have students group the religions as either Semitic or Indian. Students should cite reasons for the placement of each religion into its category.

3. Conduct an analysis of the information on the chart. Ask students to:
   - define patterns or trends between and among the religions;
   - identify rules that are pervasive and constitute ethical standards;
   - describe the major religions from different points of view (observant, religious person, agnostic, atheist, and so forth).

4. Have students define the words listed in part one of *Gandhi, the Meek Man Who Moved Millions* Study Starter, (part two will be completed later).

Teacher Notes

- Emphasize that Judaism, Christianity, and Islam share some beliefs about God along with religious history. All three share teachings from the Old Testament, while Christianity and Islam both share teachings from the New Testament. Abraham is a key figure in all three religions.
- Islam is the second largest religion in the world after Christianity, and it is also the fastest growing religion.
- Hinduism is the oldest living religion in the world, and Buddhism and Hinduism share many religious beliefs and teachings.
- Share some traditions of these religions. (examples: praying toward Mecca (Islam); the practice of vegetarianism (Hinduism); the use of Mantras or chants for prayer (Buddhism); lighting of the Menorah (Judaism); baptism (Christianity).

| Major Religions | | | | | |
Religion	Founder	Deity(ies)	Place of Worship	Beliefs	Writings
Judaism					
Christianity					
Islam					
Buddhism					
Hinduism					

- Discuss the definitions students have written for the vocabulary words on the study starter. Clarify definitions students do not understand.

5. Share the information in the Teacher Notes (at right) with the class.

- Introduce the statements, "Gandhi was a political leader, not a religious leader." Ask students to formulate a response or to take a position about the statement and support it with evidence.

- Use the following media references to augment the narrative given to students:
—Video—*Heroes & Tyrants: Gandhi*; and
—Video—*Gandhi*, starring Ben Kingsley.

Teacher Notes

India (the actual Indian name being *Bharat* for an ancient king who lived over 3,000 years ago) had been under foreign rule for many centuries. It is a country whose major religion is Hinduism, yet the country has large populations of Moslems and Sikhs. The British, whose state religion is Christianity, ruled India from the time of the last Mogul until 1948. The India of today has 23 states and 8 territories with 23 different languages. There is not even one standard calendar for all the states. By completing several tasks, you will discover how one man, Mohandas K. Gandhi, was the pivotal force to bring home rule, *Hind Swaraj*, to all of India. Although in conflict with the British government (British Raj), Gandhi managed to help India win the conflict with a minimal amount of physical contact through *satyagraha*, "holding to the truth," and *ahimsa*, "noninjury of living things." By holding fast to Hindu and Indian traditions while incorporating beliefs and teachings of religions from Christianity to Islam along with secular beliefs, Gandhi formed a philosophy that was both religious and political in nature.

6. Instruct half of the class to create a timeline or chronology of Gandhi's development as one of India's greatest leaders. Select another religious or political leader for the other half of the class to investigate. Compare the emergence of Gandhi to this other leader. Ask students to define the patterns and trends that facilitated or inhibited the emergence of each individual's leadership. Introduce a formatted chart with the purpose of determining the relationship between religious and secular beliefs of each leader that caused events leading to significant change (note: change may be positive or negative). Use the completed chart as a backdrop with students to discuss political leadership. For example, how do religious beliefs combine with secular beliefs to bring about political change? How does the religious leadership of Moses compare to the leadership of Gandhi?

Leader	Religious Belief	Secular Belief	Cause	Effect
Oliver Cromwell	Superiority of faith to good works; salvation by God's grace	Kings do not rule by "Divine Right"; Magna Carta	Civil war, beheading of the king	Establishment of Protectorate

7. Discuss the meaning of the following statement made by Gandhi.
   "All religions are true, and all religions have some error in them. … I am a Hindu, a Moslem, a Christian, and a Jew. … I want the cultures of all lands to be blown about my house as freely as possible. But, I refuse to be blown off my feet."
   Have students write a brief explanation of the quote to tell why it is meaningful. Relate the selected quote to the trends of the time—the context. Answer the question: How does the meaning of the quote relate to the time, or how does the quote transcend the times?

8. Introduce students to the concept that Gandhi admired Jesus, but believed that God had many voices, not just one. Make a class list of some of the religious beliefs or traditions that Gandhi incorporated into his own personal philosophy. Be sure to label the origin of each item on the list. Generalize from the list a big idea or theory about contemporary religion.

9. Discuss the concept that Gandhi not only incorporated several different religious beliefs and philosophies into his teachings, he also read and made use of the secular philosophies of two American authors, Henry David Thoreau and Ralph Waldo Emerson. Research these two authors. Write a synopsis of the writings from which Gandhi drew his inspiration and show their influence on Gandhi's beliefs.

10. Write a biographical sketch, either independently or in groups, about each of the following individuals in order to discuss the role each played in Gandhi's life.
   • Muhammad Ali Jinnah
   • Jawaharlal Nehru
   • Kasturbai
   • Rabindranath Tagore
   • Sir Stafford Cripps
   • Lord Mountbatten
   Once students share biographical sketches, use the information to determine:
   • how Gandhi waged "war";

- traditions and beliefs Gandhi wanted either to retain or abolish and the rationale underlying these decisions; and
- the ethical issues that emerged from the interactions among Gandhi and these people.

11. Introduce the students to the different roles of academicians—philosopher, anthropologist, and sociologist. Discuss the importance of the language of the disciplines. Have students complete part two of the study starter, *Gandhi, The Meek Man Who Moved Millions.*

12. Ask students why symbols are important to religion. What are some religious symbols for the major religions? (Responses may include: Judaism—Betzah, egg, symbolizes new life or beginning; Christianity—Icthus, Greek word for fish contains the first letters of Jesus Christ, the fish was used as a secret symbol by early Christians who feared persecution; Islam—the crescent and star believed by some to have no religious significance, the crescent is associated with Islam's lunar calendar, stars because the Koran speaks of stars as one of Allah's signs; Hinduism—the swastika is an ancient symbol of good fortune and represents the eternal wheel of life, which rotates upon an unchanging center, God; Buddhism—the bodhi tree is where the Buddha reached nirvana).

Ask students to identify symbols that Gandhi chose to represent his ideas and beliefs in order to unify the Indian people during the conflict with the British for independence.

Answer these questions: Why did Gandhi choose these symbols? What was their significance? How did the choice of symbols reflect the traditions of the Indian people? What effect did the symbols have in motivating the masses of Indian people? How did these symbols represent the overriding ideas of *satyagraha* and *ahimsa*?

Teacher Notes

The swastika was an auspicious symbol for Hindus long before the Nazis adopted it during WWII. The Nazi swastika faces a direction opposite of the swastika used by the Hindus.

◆ Output

1. Prepare a set of "character cards" to distribute to students. On 5" x 7" index cards, write the following names and identifications of each person identified as a significant individual in the life and work of Gandhi.
   - **Muhammad Ali Jinnah**—leader of the Moslem Indians, in favor of creating a separate Moslem state.
   - **Jawaharlal Nehru**—friend and supporter of Gandhi, first prime minister of India.
   - **Mohandas K. Gandhi**—the "Mahatma," the driving force behind hind swaraj for India.
   - **Rabindranath Tagore**—Nobel-prize winning poet.
   - **Godse**—editor of a newspaper, a Hindu of the Brahman caste, assassinated Gandhi.
   - **G. D. Birla**—one of Gandhi's millionaire supporters in India.
   - **Kasturbai**—Gandhi's wife.

- **harijan**—a Hindu Untouchable, harijans were declared "Children of God" by Gandhi.
- **Abdul Ghaffar Khan**—a leader of the Pathans, people who lived near the Khyber pass, these fierce fighters used force to try to control the mountain passes following the creed of "an eye for an eye, a tooth for a tooth."
- **a *ryot***—a peasant who lives in one of India's 700,000 villages.
- **Sir Stafford Cripps**—sent by the British Raj to negotiate with Indian leaders during WWII.
- **Winston Churchill**—prime minister of England who refused to receive a visit from Gandhi.
- **General Smuts**—British governor of South Africa.
- **Lord Irvin**—British viceroy of India during the Salt March.
- **Lord Mountbatten**—India's last, and most responsive, viceroy.
- **King George and Queen Mary**—Gandhi called on the royal couple during his visit to Great Britain.
- **a worker at the textile mill in Lancashire, England**—Gandhi stayed in the poorer sections of England and visited workers in the textile mills.
- **Louis Fischer**—an American journalist who followed Gandhi on his campaign throughout India.

2. Distribute a character card to individual, pairs, or small groups of students. Describe the concept of a round-table discussion wherein students:
   - research the character assigned to them;
   - plan the costume depicting the character in time and place;
   - decorate a name tag to symbolize the individual being portrayed in the round-table discussion so viewers can identify the discussants by the roles they are assuming; and
   - participate in a round-table discussion by assuming the persona of the character.

3. Stage the round-table discussion with students taking on the personas of their assigned characters/personalities. Arrange desks in a large circle. Students will then place their nametags on the desks in front of them. Identify a moderator by assigning a student to the task or let the teacher assume the moderator's role. The moderator will start the discussion by reading the first questions/statement and randomly asking one of the characters to respond. Participants may respond to each other's statements at any time by reflecting the beliefs of the personas they represent.

4. Use the following list of topics to stimulate the round table discussion;
   - Home rule for India; reality or unrealistic dream?
   - The only way to gain independence is through physical force.
   - India cannot live as one country; partition is necessary.
   - The British have given India many gifts such as railways, postal service, telegraph, public works, and irrigation systems.
   - India needs the Raj to improve the lives of its peoples.
   - Conflict can lead to both positive and negative effects.

◆ Culmination

1. Look in newspapers and magazines, listen to radio or television news programs, or use the Internet to find out as much as you can about the India of today.

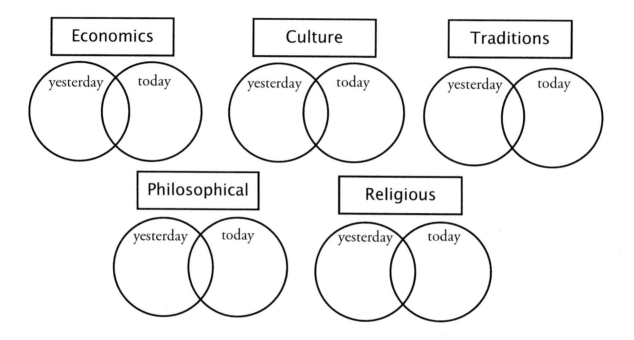

*   Create a series of Venn Diagrams showing the similarities and differences of India today compared to India in the time of Gandhi.
*   Conduct a class discussion using the information students have gathered for their sets of Venn Diagrams. Questions for the discussion may include:
    — What cultural traditions or beliefs are no longer followed to a great extent? Why did differences in traditions change over time?
    — What is the relationship between the Hindus and Moslems of today? Has that relationship changed since India was fighting for hind swaraj?
    — How are Gandhi's beliefs and ideals still at work in India today? Why have some beliefs faded while others are prominent?
    — How has the quality of life changed for the people of India? Where can the influence of other cultures and religions be seen in India today?
    — What would India be like today if there had been no Gandhi? What would life be like if Gandhi had not been assassinated? How can Gandhi's beliefs be applied to societies in the world today?
    — What conflicts have emerged either to change or maintain the culture's status quo?

◆ Extensions

—Independent Research Topic

1. Discuss the concept of stereotyping. Relate the discussion to religious stereotyping as expressed in the statement, "All Moslems are Arabs." Discuss how misconceptions and

bad feelings result from stereotyping. Gather a list of these stereotypical ideas relating to cultures, traditions, and religion. Create a pamphlet or poster that refutes some stereotypical ideas.

2. Historically, women have not been given high status or have been excluded from different aspects of religious life. Find religions in which women have not been excluded and may even have been given high status. Create a poster report detailing the role of women in the religion you researched.

3. Defend or refute one of the following statements;
   * Religious beliefs hamper creative expression.
   * Religion favors family life.
   * Intense religious beliefs create extremism and cults.
   * Strong religious beliefs are essential for personal autonomy.
   * Religious belief causes conflict.

4. Examine the ethical teachings of several different religions. Create a chart that shows the many commonalities of these teachings.

5. Defend the concept that religious charities often are given permission to work in areas that would be forbidden to others, such as war zones. Learn about a religious charity such as the Salvation Army or Moslem Aid. Create a campaign to raise money so that the organization can continue to perform its good works.

6. Examine the concept that many people's religious beliefs are entwined with nature. The aborigines of Australia believed that people could not own nature. Nature was part of the cycle of life. Research how the aboriginal religious beliefs created conflict with the British colonists. Write a letter as an aboriginal leader to the colonists explaining your religious beliefs and action.

7. Research the relationship between modern-day languages and Sanskrit. Sanskrit is known to be a mathematical language. Find out how Stanford University is researching Sanskrit for use with computers. Use Internet sources for this research.

8. Research the influence of Hindu and Indian iconography on the world of art. Compare and contrast the use of icons by other religions.

9. Research a selection of religious art. Define how religious art is both an expression of artistic skill and religious beliefs. Create a tour of one or more religious art forms to prove the relationship between art and religious beliefs.

—Classical Connection: Philosophy

The British philosopher John Stuart Mill stated that "To deny others the right to express their opinions is to assume one's own infallibility." Discuss the statement with students, then ask students to apply the idea to the British in India and to other countries and situations, especially current events. How might the British (or other group in control) respond to the statement? Written responses, oral presentations, and role playing are possible outcome activities.

— Adaptations for Other Grade Levels

Use the American Civil Rights Movement and the work of Dr. Martin Luther King, Jr., in order to show the relationship between religious and secular beliefs as a powerful tool for change and non-violent conflict.

Gandhi, the Meek Man Who Moved Millions

Part One: Language of the Study

Define the following terms and then use them as the **language** of studying Gandhi by using the words as descriptors or **details** of his life.

civil disobedience	hartal	hind swaraj
bapu	Mahatma	ashrams
fasting	ahimsa	satyagraha
caste system	Brahmans	Kshatriyas
Vaisyas	Sudras	harijans
suttee	Bhagavad Gita	partitioning of India

Part Two: Examine the Life of Gandhi

Assume the role of an academician to discuss one or all of these topics as they relate to Gandhi's life.

1. Relationship between religious and secular beliefs.

2. The media as a tool for change.

3. Religious leaders: yesterday, today, and the future.

Religious Icon Foil Relief

Religious art can be a powerful force in society.

Religious icons are evident throughout the history of humankind. These icons served as tools for communicating. Often, the icons were used to communicate in secrecy. Nonbelievers were unaware of the meanings behind the symbols. Art historians have given us tremendous insight through their knowledge of iconography, the skill of interpreting an artifact through the study of its symbols, subject matter, and theme. Throughout art history, religious icons have appeared in many forms and in many media. With regard to Christianity, icons appeared in the forms of paintings, mosaics, sculptures, and relief sculptures. In the early days of Christianity, Christians would draw icons in the sand in clandestine meetings. The use of icons has remained a vital part of our culture today.

Objective

The students will create an aluminum foil relief based on a design of religious icons. The completed artifact will have the appearance of an antique tooled metal design.

Materials

- art history books
- student research on religion
- Internet research
- 9" x 12" drawing paper
- pencils
- scissors
- ball point pen
- cardboard or matboard cut to dimensions not to exceed 9" x 12"
- heavy duty aluminum foil
- liquid white glue
- scraps of poster board
- spools of twine or jute
- 1½" to 2" paint brush
- one bottle of India ink
- newspaper
- plastic bowls
- steel wool or plastic scouring pad

Procedure

1. Decide on the dimensions of this project. You may choose to use either a square or a rectangular format. Cut the drawing paper and the cardboard. Draw the design consisting of a religious icon theme onto the drawing paper.

2. This project is a relief, a three-dimensional object projecting from a flat surface. The depth of this relief should not exceed ¼" from the surface of the cardboard.

3. Once the design is drawn on paper, the student must decide which parts of the design will be raised in the relief. If the student has drawn an object such as a cross, it can be cut out of a piece of cardboard and glued onto the precut cardboard, or the student might choose to raise only the outline of the cross by gluing a line of jute onto the cardboard. The results would be very different. One cross would appear to be a cross that is completely raised from the background, and the other would appear to be a raised outline of a cross.

4. The student then creates a three-dimensional likeness of the design by cutting pieces of cardboard, poster board, and jute or twine and gluing the parts onto the cardboard background.

5. Once the composition is glued in place and dry, cut the aluminum foil. Add 4 inches to both dimensions of the cardboard background. If the cardboard measures 6" x 6", the aluminum foil should measure 10" x 10".

6. Crumple the aluminum foil. Now open and flatten the sheet. It should have a wrinkled appearance.

7. Place the wrinkled foil so that the shiny side is faced down. Cover the dull side with the white glue. Use a scrap of poster board to smear the glue onto the entire surface of the aluminum foil. Be sure to cover the work area with newspaper or other material to protect the surface of the desks or tables.

8. Place the aluminum foil over the cardboard relief and gradually press it onto it. Start applying pressure in the middle of the composition and work outward. Wrap excess foil under the sides of the relief.

9. Continue to apply pressure to the design until the relief design begins to show. A pencil eraser can work as well as fingers. Once the task is done, begin to add texture to any part of the surface that needs it. Use a ball-point pen or blunt pencil point to draw little hatching lines, tiny circles, or dots. This will give the relief the appearance of metal tooling. Should the foil tear, do not be concerned. Simply press the foil down to secure it.

10. The next step requires India ink. This ink is permanent if it gets on clothing, but, it will wash off of hands. This step is important because it will give the relief the antique appearance and conceal any holes or tears in the foil. Apply the India ink onto the foil until it sticks. Let it dry and then remove the ink with steel wool or a plastic scouring pad. The ink will remain in the textured areas of the relief design, which will give the icon relief an antique appearance.

Evaluation

Did the student produce a metallic relief that appears to be an antique? Did the student demonstrate care for craftsmanship? Is the overall composition aesthetically pleasing?

Art Reference Books

The Art Book (1998). London: Phaidon.

Janson, H. W. (1997). *The history of art.* New York: H. Abrams.

Strickland, C. & Boswell, J. (1992). *The annotated Mona Lisa: A crash course in art history from prehistoric to postmodern.* Kansas City: Andrews & McNeel.

Tansey, R. (1995). *Gardner's art through the ages.* New York: HBJ.

Probability & Statistics:
Collecting Data

I. Teacher Preparation

◆ Background
Time Required: 6–8 class periods

Getting Ready
For this lesson you will need the following:
- various types of charts of statistical data; and
- Internet access.

Curriculum Standards

The student will:

Primary Standard
- Use appropriate statistical representations to analyze data.

Embedded Content and Skills
- Apply mathematics to solve problems connected to everyday experiences, investigations in other disciplines, and activities inside and outside of school.

Curriculum Standard Level:
Introductory   **Developmental X**   Extension

◆ Framework

Theme: Conflict

Generalization: Varying relationships create varying types of conflict. Conflict may allow for synthesis and change. Conflict may be natural or human-made.

Content Focus: Probability and Statistics—Students will look at statisticians from various disciplines to see how they collect and use data.

Rationale: The study of probability and statistics gives students insight into how different disciplines use data.

Differentiation Framework

Thinking Skills	Depth/Complexity	Research	Products
• Identify attributes • Compare/contrast • Gather evidence to support • Summarize • State assumptions	• Details • Patterns • Rules • Different perspectives	• Internet resources • Media resources • Reference books • Interview	• Graphs • Presentations

Thinking Skills

- **Identify attributes**—describe qualities and characteristics.
  Example: Students will identify the characteristics of different types of graphs.
- **Compare and contrast**—note similarities and differences.
  Example: Students will compare and contrast graphs and statistical methods of communication.
- **Summarize**—understanding main ideas.
  Example: Students will summarize their research.
- **State assumptions**—explaining underlying concepts.
  Example: Students will state their assumptions about how and why statistics and graphs are used.

Depth/Complexity

- **Details**—parts, attributes, factors, and variables.
  Example: Students will use details to explain the structure and purpose of graphs.
- **Patterns**—repetition; predictability.
  Example: Students will note recurring patterns and trends in the use of statistical information.
- **Rules**—structure, order, and hierarchy.

Example: Students will define the rules applicable to using, interpreting, and presenting statistical information.

- **Different perspectives**—multiple perspectives, opposing viewpoints, differing roles and knowledge.

  Example: Students will compare and contrast statistical data and graphs for roles of professional disciplinarians.

Research

Students will use a variety of reference resources, including the Internet, media resources, books, and interviews, to gather data for debate.

Product

Students will present results in the form of charts, photo essays, and/or dramatizations based on controversial issues from history and current events.

II. The Lesson

◆ Motivation

1. Present four different types of graphs depicting statistical data communicating topics from various disciplines. (See Web site: http://www.amstat.org/education/careers.html— also see Teacher Notes for other sources.)
2. Ask the students to compare and contrast these graphs and state their assumptions about what and how each graph communicates.
3. Record the students' ideas on a chart for later reference.
4. Ask the students to generate questions about the structure and purpose of the graphs. Possible questions that students may ask:
   - What does this graph show?
   - How does the form or structure of the graph affect communication of statistical data?
   - How do you think this information was collected?
   - What determines the relationship between the type of data and the appropriateness of the type of graph used to present the data?
5. Record the students' questions on a separate chart.

◆ Input

Teacher Notes

If the students have a question about where the chart came from, then the teacher would ask, "Where could this chart have come from? Let's see, since the chart is labeled 'Consumer Products' and the products that are listed are computer-related, I can assume that this chart was used to record information about computer products. This leads me to think about the following question: What type of person or disciplinarian would need to collect data such as this and for what purpose?"

This line of thinking aloud would continue until the teacher has exhausted the questions that the students had recorded on the chart.

1. Use the questions and one example of a graph to demonstrate how the questions can be answered in a metacognitive manner or method. (See Teacher Notes on page 56.)

2. Summarize the demonstration by informing the students that, because of the world's increasing use of data for prediction and decision making, it is important that people understand the purposes and processes used in collecting and analyzing data. The task of a statistician is to collect, organize, and describe data systematically. Statisticians analyze data in a variety of ways: graph-ically, numerically, looking for patterns, trends, and unusual observations.

3. Solicit answers to the remainder of the questions on the list of original questions. Reintroduce the variety of graphs. Remind students that the graphs are from several different disciplines and use various forms of recording data. Answer generated questions.

4. Summarize the responses about graphing into a set of rules or principles. Validate these rules or principles with information from the curriculum standards.

◆ Output

Present the students with a list of various disciplinarians, including computer-systems technician, accountant, environmental scientist, management consultant, sociologist, mathematician, media specialist, anthropologist, sociologist, psychologist, and professionals in education, insurance, government, business, medicine, banking, and telecommunications. Assign disciplinarians to individuals or small groups to research. Inform students that they must define the "patterns of use" relating to collecting and interpreting statistical data with graphs. Conduct a comparative analysis of how disciplinarians use graphs. (See Research Requirements Study Starter.)

◆ Culmination

Teacher Notes

Make sure that the charts are varied in style—pie chart, bar graph, stem and leaf plot, and so forth. The following Web sites are sources for statistical charts.

- http://www.census.gov/statab/www/graphs.html
- http://www.census.gov/statab/www/img/occ.gif —fastest growing occupations
- http://www.census.gov/statab/www/img/wage.gif —average earnings of year-round full-time workers in 1992
- http://www.census.gov/statab/www/img/soft.gif— microcomputer software sales 1993
- http://www.census.gov/statab/www/img/health.gif —persons without health insurance in 1990–93
- http://www.census.gov/statab/www/img/smoke.gif —cigarette smokers in 1992
- http://www.census.gov/statab/www/img/expends. gif—consumer expenditures in 1992

Examples of statistical careers: computer-systems technician, insurance, government, banking, accounting, telecommunications, environmental science, management consulting, sociologist, mathematician, education, media-related fields, anthropology, sociology, psychology, law, business, and medicine.

1. Present the two generalizations about conflict. (See Prove or Verify the Meaning of Two Generalizations Study Starter.)
   - Conflict may allow for synthesis and change.
   - Conflict may be natural or human-made.
2. Instruct students to use the information they collected about professional disciplinarians and their use and presentation of statistical data in order to prove or verify the generalizations.
3. Create a class graph to depict the relationship between the work of disciplinarians and professionals and the methods of collecting, interpreting, and presenting the data.

◆ **Extensions**
—Independent Research
Research the role of statistical data in influencing people to "buy," "vote," or "join."

—Interdisciplinary Options
Research the concept "numbers lie" as it relates to an historical event, solution to a problem in a story or novel, incentive for funding in science, or promotion of a scientific discovery. Summarize issues of *conflict* that originate using numbers to communicate ideas. Research the same problem or issue from the perspectives of two different disciplinarians. Determine how the purposes and patterns of their roles affect the interpretations and presentation of data.

Situation	Disciplines
Genetic Engineering	Medicine vs. Law
	Business vs. Environmentalist
Rain Forest Deforestation	Medicine vs. Business
	Business vs. Environmentalist
HMO Providers	Insurance vs. Medicine
Mergers	Banking vs. Small Business
Computer Access	Computer Technology vs. Psychology
School Board Policies	Education vs. Government
War	Government vs. Media

—Classical Connections
Study the most recent U.S. census and the census of William the Conqueror. Compare and contrast differences in collecting statistical data and how the data was or will be used. Relate the findings to the generalizations about conflict.

Research Requirements

1. Title of discipline.

2. Locate two graphs of different forms (pie chart, bar graph, etc.) in the field of the discipline.

3. Describe the data on these graphs by identifying the attributes. Use the language of a statistician when describing the data. For example: *mean, median, mode,* and *range*.

4. Compare and contrast the two graphs.

5. How was the information gathered?

6. What is the purpose for the collection of this data?

7. What are the detail, patterns, and rules found in the statistics of this discipline?

8. Summarize your findings.

9. State assumptions about using statistics in this discipline.

Prove or Verify the Meaning of Two Generalizations

1. What is the relationship of the facts or concepts you studied about statistics to the generalization? What information do you have that supports or verifies one or more of the generalizations?

2. Place the information you researched (a) in the dotted space supporting a single generalization or (b) in the dotted space that supports both generalizations. Explain the decision you have made to place the information in a particular location.

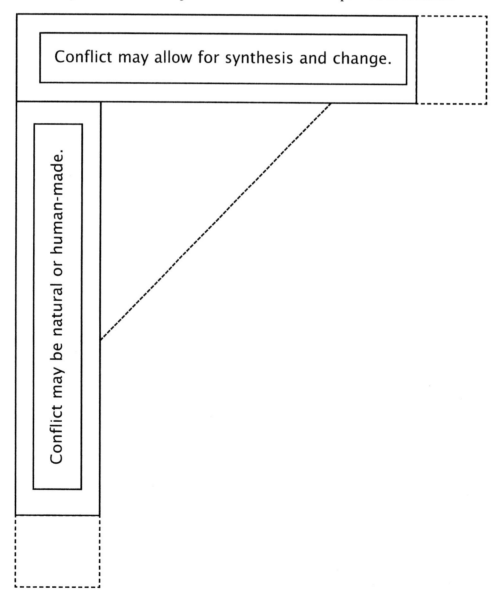

Conflict may allow for synthesis and change.

Conflict may be natural or human-made.

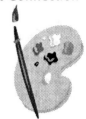

Designing a House

Architecture is a synthesis of the sometimes conflicting elements of mathematics, construction, and art.

Architecture, the art, science, or profession of designing and constructing buildings and other functional structures, has a history that dates back to the earliest times. Today, when we think of outstanding architectural achievements, we think of colossal monoliths such as the Sears Tower in Chicago. Across the oceans are ancient structural phenomena like the Taj Mahal in India, the Egyptian pyramids of Mycerinus, Chefren, and Cheops at Giza, Egypt, and the Cathedral of Notre Dame in Paris, France. Each of these amazing human achievements was designed with a purpose, to fulfill a function for humankind.

Architecture plays an integral part of our lives today as it has in the past. We reside, work, play, learn, shop, and receive medical care in architectural forms. Architects create these buildings through an ever-changing art form that is highly influenced by science, technology, the environment, economics, cultures, and aesthetic trends.

Architects must be concerned with the interior and exterior design of a structure, as well as integral parts that make a building suitable for human habitation, such as lighting, plumbing, and overall space. Their careers are challenging and constantly changing. Today's architecture must reflect a conscientious concern for environmental impact. Energy conservation is an important issue. This concern influences the materials used, and that in turn can affect the appearance of the structure. In New Mexico, for example, architects are designing buildings, some of them houses, using adobe, a material that has been used by Native Americans of the region for hundreds of years. Its use is highly energy efficient because buildings built with adobe stay cool in hot desert temperatures during daylight hours and comfortably warm when night falls. Aside from its practical use, adobe buildings have a distinctive aesthetic appeal that is uniquely southwestern.

Objective

The students will collaborate in groups of three or four to design a house based on the accumulation of data regarding the needs of the buyer.

Materials

- magazines that contain floor plans
- rulers
- compasses
- pencils and pencil sharpeners
- large sheets of white paper 18" x 24" (white butcher paper)
- ruled paper
- books on building materials
- graphing paper

Procedure

1. Put students in groups of three or four. Brainstorm the items that an architect will incorporate in the design of a house. Compile a list that each group will use.

2. Each group will decide on the specifications for their house. How many bedrooms will it have? Will it have a game room or swimming pool? Some of the specifications can be closets, doors, windows, bathrooms, kitchen, lighting, garage, patio, porch, landscaping, and foyer. These are simply suggestions. After viewing floor plans from magazines, the students will grasp the idea.

3. Establish the scale of the drawing. Will each linear foot be represented by a quarter inch or a half inch? The students should gather measurements of doors, halls, ceilings, windows, and garage doors.

4. Decide on the geographic location of the house because this will affect the materials used to build it. Will the house be facing north, south, east, or west?

5. Once all of the data is accumulated, the students will begin to draw the house. Rooms should be drawn on the graphing paper. The rooms can be cut out and then arranged and rearranged on the white paper until the final floor plan is achieved. Finalize the floor plan by neatly drawing all lines with a ruler and labeling each area of the house.

Evaluation

Did the floor plan meet the needs of the home buyer? Was the design well executed?

Art Reference Books

The art book. (1998). London: Phaidon.

Janson, H. W. (1997). *The history of art.* New York: H. Abrams.

Strickland, C. & Boswell, J. (1992). *The annotated Mona Lisa: A crash course in art history from prehistoric to postmodern.* Kansas City: Andrews & McNeel.

Tansey, R. (1995). *Gardner's art through the ages.* New York: HBJ.

It's in the Genes!

I. Teacher Preparation

◆ **Background**
Time Required: 8 class periods

Getting Ready
For this lesson you will need the following:
* a copy of "Race is Over: Black, White, Red, Yellow—same difference" *New York Times Magazine*, Sept. 29, 1996;
* *Drosophila* lab materials; and
* photos of Louise Nevelson assemblages.

Curriculum Standards

The student will:

Primary Standard
* Know that the present form and function of species results from gradual or sporadic change.

Embedded Content and Skills
* Conduct field and laboratory investigations using safe, environmentally appropriate, and ethical practices.
* Use scientific inquiry methods during field and laboratory investigations.
* Use critical thinking and scientific problem solving to make informed decisions.
* Use a variety of tools and methods to conduct science inquiry.

Curriculum Standard Level:
Introductory   **Developmental X**   Extension

◆ Framework

Theme: Conflict

Generalization: Conflict can be a necessary component for change.

Content Focus: Genetics—the branch of biology that deals with the heredity and variation of organisms.

Rationale: Understanding the mechanics of inherited traits is important if students are to comprehend the more complex system of genetics and its biological and social implications.

Differentiation Framework

Thinking Skills	Depth/Complexity	Research	Products
• Test assumptions	• Language of discipline • Details • Ethics • Different perspectives	• Conduct experiments • Text sources	• Biographical sketch

Thinking Skills

- **Test assumptions**—to determine validity of prior concepts.
  Example: Students will test assumptions about inherited traits as they design experiments to prove their hypotheses about assimilation of species.

Depth/Complexity

- **Language of the discipline**—the specialized vocabulary, tools used by the discipline.
  Example: Students will use language appropriate to the work of a geneticist.
- **Details**—basic facts, ideas, and concepts of the discipline.
  Example: Students will systematically record facts in an experimental situation.
- **Ethics**—different opinions; judging.
  Example: Students will consider the ideas of conflict in racial matters.
- **Different perspectives**—examining the same topic from more than one point of view.
  Example: Students will examine the idea of genetic change from the perspective of economists and physicians.

Research

- **Conduct experiments**—draw conclusions based on observation of controlled events.
  Example: Students will design and conduct experiments with drosophila to understand elements of genetic change.
- **Text resources**—variety of text and media information.

Example: Students will use a number of text sources to gather information on genetic variation.

Product

Students will create a biographical and visual sketch of an American in the year 2100.

II. The Lesson

◆ Motivation

1. Introduce the concepts associated with genetics using the *New York Times* article: "Race is Over: Black, White, Red, Yellow—same difference." *The New York Times Magazine*, Sep 29, 1996 p170 col 1 [24 col in.] by Stanley Crouch. Teacher may read the article to the class or have students read the article independently or in small discussion groups (see summary on page 67).

2. Have the students make a list of their unanswered questions related to the article. Keep a list of the questions on a chart. Questions can be generated as a whole-class activity or in small discussion groups.

3. Analyze the list of questions. Identify those questions that relate to conflict as a component of change. Circle, highlight, or underline these key questions. These questions will be used as references throughout the lesson.

◆ Input

1. Conduct an investigation of genetic change, using either the following or another lab (see Study Starter, Traits: a Family Matter).
    *   *Red Eyes to White Eyes in Drosophila Flies.* Look for inheritance patterns in three generations. This lab takes about 30 days, with days 1, 10, and 20 taking about 45 minutes each. Other days will need about 15 minutes to maintain control of the project. This investigation should be underway before beginning this lesson. (Information for conducting the drosophila investigation can be found in textbooks, including *Addison Wesley: Life Science Laboratory Manual,* 1989).

2. Use evidence based on observations from the lab to revisit and answer the questions posted previously on the charts. Answer as many questions as possible. Add new questions that arise.

3. Identify ethical issues in genetics after completing the scientific inquiry. List these on a chart.

4. Use this chart to analyze the issues from the following points of view: historian, futurist, physician, economist, theologian, and expectant parents.

Concepts in Genetics	Ethical issues
genetic engineering	*unknown consequences*

◆ Output

Based on the information from the ethical issues chart, use the geneticist's perspective to prove that conflict is necessary for change.

Genetic · · · · Conflict Change

—*Example: Physical characteristics separate the races now. In the future, these characteristics will become less prominent, making racial distinctions less noticeable.*

◆ Culmination

Create a biographical sketch to represent an American in the year 2100.

1. Provide portraits of many people from many cultures for students to describe and compare. Have students note differences and similarities in facial characteristics and skin color.

2. Using the conclusions from the lab, have the students create a sketch, either in a drawing or with words, of an American in the year 2100. Students need to provide evidence that supports their sketch with data from the lab (e.g., dominant and recessive genes, etc.). Students need to provide evidence that supports their sketch with three to four generations from:
   - Punnett Squares showing at least three characteristics such as hair color, hair texture, eye color, eye shape, skin tone, and nose shape (Punnett Square Study Starter); and
   - pedigree charts showing at least three characteristics (same as above).

3. Present sketches to the class speaking from a futurist geneticist's point of view.

◆ Extensions
—Independent Research Topics

Provide students with the following list of topics:

1. Inherited traits associated with certain ethnic groups.
2. Isolation of specific genes.
   - Examples include genes for aggression, obesity, sickle-cell, achondroplasia, PKU.
3. Cloning.

Teacher Notes

Cell—a small, microscopic mass of protoplasm bounded externally by a semipermeable membrane, usually including one or more nuclei and various non-living products, capable alone or interacting with other cells of performing all the fundamental functions of life and forming the least structural unit of living matter capable of functioning independently.

DNA—deoxyribonucleic acid. Any of various nucleic acids that are localized especially in cell nuclei, are the molecular basis of heredity in many organisms, and are constructed of a double helix held together by hydrogen bonds between purine and pyrimidine bases that project inward from two chains containing alternate links of deoxyribose and phosphate.

Miscegenation—the mixture of races; especially marriage between a white person and a member of another race.

Assimilation—the merging of cultural traits from previously distinct cultural populations.

Genome—a map of the location of individual genes on every chromosome of an individual.

4. Choosing traits and characteristics of unborn children in the future.
5. Human Genome Study.

—Interdisciplinary Options

1. Trace the development of a multicultural society in the United States by creating food, clothing, literature, architecture, art, and music collages to depict the "melting pot" or "salad" concepts of our heterogeneous populations. Label the collages by time (date) and place (state or city). Consider dividing the class into groups so that each group can illustrate a particular time and place. Arrange the collages in chronological and/or place order. Discuss the progression of multiculturalism in our society.

2. Select a particular hyphenated American culture or racial group. Describe (1) the origin of the group's presence in the United States; (2) the group's methods of assimilation; (3) the degree of the group's assimilation; and (4) the predictions about the group's influence in American society of the future.

—Classical Connections

Investigate the categorization of multiracial individuals by using the U.S. Census Bureau data.

Article Summary

"Race is Over: Black, White, Red, Yellow—Same Difference." by Stanley Crouch. *New York Times Magazine,* September 29, 1996.

The author predicts that, within the next 100 years, the concept of separate races will have ceased to be important. Using examples of individuals of mixed parentage (Finnish/African American, Dominican/Russian-Jewish, African American/Filipino/American Indian/French Canadian, etc.), Crouch contends that intermarriage will blur distinctions between groups of people. Cultural borrowing is another factor that in the past has enriched society, and the article argues that it will become more prevalent in the future. In addition, he holds that members of what are today separate groups will cease to see an attachment to the elements of group identity worth being self-excluded from mainstream culture.

TRAITS:
A FAMILY MATTER

In this investigation, you will make observations of your own physical traits and those of your parents and grandparents.

1. Complete the chart below with the student's own phenotype.

Characteristic	Dominant	Recessive	Your Phenotype
1. hair texture	curly	straight	
2. hair whorl	clockwise	counter	
3. hair color	brown/black	blonde/red	
4. hair at forehead	widow's peak	none	
5. eyelashes	long	short	
6. nose	turned up	not turned up	
7. ear lobes	free	attached	
8. tongue	can roll	can't roll	
9. eye color	dark	blue, green	
10. eye shape	large	small	
11. freckles	yes	no	
12. skin tones	dark	light	

2. Complete the chart below with information about your parents and grandparents.

Characteristic	Parents' Phenotypes		Grandparents' Phenotype			
	1	2	1	2	3	4
1. hair texture						
2. hair whorl						
3. hair color						
4. hair at forehead						
5. eyelashes						
6. nose						
7. ear lobes						
8. tongue						
9. eye color						
10. eye shape						
11. freckles						
12. skin tones						

- Can you tell from whom you received your phenotypes for each of these traits?
- What conclusions can you draw about inherited traits?

Punnett Squares: Making Predictions

An easy way to predict the genetic results of a cross between two parents is to draw a Punnett Square. Each box contains one of the possible combinations of genes for one trait inherited from the parents. Punnett Squares can help predict the numbers of different phenotypes produced by a certain cross.

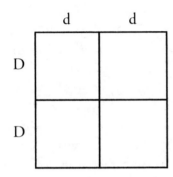

The letters on the left represent the possible genes in the sex cells of one parent (in this case, dominate DD: dark haired).

The letters on the top show the possible genes in the sex cells of the other parent (in this case, recessive dd: light haired).

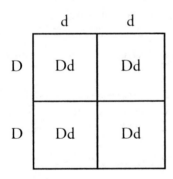

After matching the possible genotypes of the offspring, the possible phenotypes can be determined. In this case all offspring will have dominate dark hair with a recessive light hair gene that may be passed on to the offspring.

In the squares below, record the genetic possibilities of three characteristics for an American in 2100.

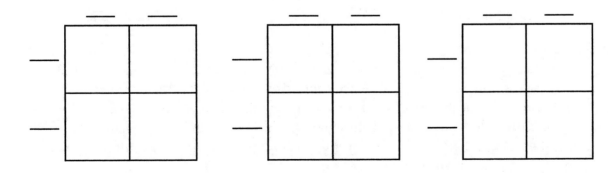

Sculpture— The Assemblage

Sculpture has evolved over the years, not unlike the adaptations in nature, altering form and material in response to cultural changes.

Modern sculpture of the second half of the 20th century was and still is highly experimental. Artists have used every imaginable media from stone to glass and steel. The medium is just another vehicle to fulfill the artist's creative needs. There are no limits regarding the choices. During this period of art, many unique artistic styles have evolved.

The assemblage technique of Louise Nevelson is one of these styles. Louise Nevelson enjoyed constructing wooden objects from an early age. Sculpting with wood hardly seems like a modern idea. After all, wood was also a favorite medium of the later Middle Ages. Nevelson's use of wood was unlike anything created before. She collected wooden boxes, discarded furniture, found objects made from wood such as baseball bats, even wooden instruments, and assembled them to create magnificent sculptures. Boxes were filled with wooden scraps and various recognizable objects. The recognizable objects retain their identity, but lose their intended function. These forms were arranged to create an assemblage, or three-dimensional collage, of more complex and interesting forms. They became magnificent nonrepresentational monuments of form, space, light, and shadow.

Louise Nevelson's assemblages were always monochromatic. A single color unified the assortment of smaller forms into one sculpted object. Later in her career, Louise Nevelson experimented with other materials such as Cor-Ten steel and aluminum. Her steel sculptures reach heights of 90 feet.

Objective
The students will collectively create an assemblage in the style of Louise Nevelson's sculptures.

Materials
- shoe boxes
- white glue
- glue gun
- large sheets of cardboard or ¼-inch or ½-inch foam board
- found objects (discarded toys, wood scraps, cans, plastic bottles, small boxes, paper egg cartons, etc.)
- can(s) of spray paint

Procedure
1. Each student will collect objects to glue inside a shoe box. The objects should fill the space within the shoe box. Use white glue or a glue gun.
2. After each student completes designing and gluing the interior of the boxes, the shoe boxes should be arranged and glued onto the sheet of cardboard or foam board.
3. Once this is done, the students will decide on the color for the assemblage. Nevelson typically used colors such as white, black, and metallic gold.

4. Spray the sculpture with the paint of the selected color. Use caution. The students should not spray the sculpture unless they are under instructor supervision and equipped with protective goggles, dust masks, and suitable clothing. This task should be done outdoors.

Evaluation

Did the students create interesting designs within the shoe box space using found objects? Was the form well-crafted?

Art Reference Books

The art book. (1998). London: Phaidon.

Janson, H. W. (1997) *The history of art.* New York: H. Abrams.

Strickland, C. & Boswell, J. (1992). *The annotated Mona Lisa: A crash course in art history from pre-historic to postmodern.* Kansas City: Andrews & McNeel.

Tansey, Richard. (1995). *Gardner's art through the ages.* New York: HBJ.

Seventh GRADE

Theme: Relationships

- Language Arts—Mysteries, We Write
- Social Studies—Diversity, A Unifying Force
- Math—Probability & Statistics: Fuel for Debate
- Science—Ecological Succession

Mysteries, We Write

I. Teacher Preparation

◆ **Background**
Time Required: 5–6 weeks

Getting Ready
For this lesson you will need the following:
- short stories by Edgar Allen Poe including "Murders in the Rue Morgue," "Purloined Letter," and "The Gold Bug";
- short stories by Sir Arthur Conan Doyle, including "Red-Headed League," "The Speckled Band," "Adventures of the Blue Carbuncle," and "The Dying Detective"; and
- colored note cards.

Curriculum Standards

The student will:

Primary Standard
- Recognize how features of a genre build understanding of the human experience.

Embedded Content and Skills
- Read classic and contemporary works.
- Find similarities and differences in treatment, scope, and organization.
- Analyze characters, including their traits, motivations, conflicts, point of view, relationships, and changes they undergo.
- Collaborate with other writers to compose, organize, and revise.
- Use effective rate, volume, pitch, and tone for the audience and setting.

Curriculum Standard Level:
Introductory   **Developmental X**   Extension

◆ Framework

Theme: Relationships

Generalization: Relationships extend over time and exist between the past and present, as well as within and across disciplines. These relationships can be discovered by using logic and reasoning. Studies of the past provide an opportunity to see its relationship to the present and to forecast the future.

Content Focus: Mystery/detective genre.

Rationale: The study of mysteries/detective stories relates to human need to establish order and logic in the everyday world. Because gifted students are curious, they enjoy solving mysteries. The desire to use logic and reasoning to explain the unknown transcends every discipline. The study of the mystery genre from its beginning to the present is, therefore, a perfect opportunity to explore the mysteries of other disciplines. It allows students to see how humankind has attempted to find relationships and patterns throughout time.

Differentiation Framework

Thinking Skills	Depth/Complexity	Research	Products
• Determine cause/effect • Think inductively • Identify ambiguity • Determine relevance	• Patterns • Language of discipline • Establish interdisciplinary connections • Changes over time	• Etymologies • Authors of detective genre • Mysteries of other disciplines	• Create a mystery • Write and perform a mystery play • Student-run seminar

Thinking Skills

- **Determine cause/effect**—to explain why certain events occur and the results of this action, activity, or event.
  Example: Students will use cause and effect to explain character motivation/conflict in writing and solving mysteries.
- **Think inductively**—to arrive at a concept generalization from a collection of facts.
  Example: Students will analyze information relating to a crime and draw conclusions based on the evidence.
- **Identify ambiguity**—to sense inconsistencies, gaps, and incongruities.
  Example: Students will solve mysteries by perceiving the ambiguities.
- **Determine relevance**—to decide the value and importance of information.
  Example: Students will decide the relevance of clues as they solve and create their own mysteries.

Depth/Complexity

- **Patterns**—repetitive action; repetitive activities.
  Example: Students will identify the patterns in mystery/detective stories.
- **Language of the discipline**—specialized vocabulary, tools used by the discipline.
  Example: Students will identify, analyze, and write mysteries, using the language of detectives/law enforcement.
- **Establish interdisciplinary connections**—relationships within, between, and across disciplines.
  Example: Students will compare the strategies used by detectives to those used by scientists, mathematicians, and others who must think inductively.
- **Changes over time**—relationships between past, present, and future; relationships within a time period.
  Example: Students will relate how the pattern of the detective story has evolved over time, as well as how various authors adapt the pattern.

Research

- Students will look up the etymology of *ratiocination* and explain its meaning.
- Students will research famous authors of the detective genre independently.

Teacher Notes

Edgar Allen Poe and Sir Arthur Conan Doyle

- Edgar Allen Poe is the father of the detective genre. His character, Auguste Dupin, is the prototype of the modern detective. The first detective story (he called it a tale of ratiocination) was "Murders in the Rue Morgue," which was published in 1841. In 1842, he published and won a $100 prize (a fair amount of money at that time) for "The Gold Bug." Many literary analysts argue that "The Gold Bug" is not a detective story because it doesn't fit the pattern.

- When Sir Arthur Conan Doyle began writing his mysteries in 1891, he patterned his detective, Sherlock Holmes, upon Dupin. After writing several volumes of his Sherlock Holmes stories, Doyle became tired of them, and he attempted to end the series with the story, "The Adventure of the Final Problem," in which Morarity killed Holmes. However, the public reaction was so strong that Doyle began writing the Holmes stories again. Distinct relationships can be seen between Poe's and Doyle's detective stories and those written subsequently.

Patterns of the Detective Story:

- Poe's definition of a tale of ratiocination (tale of reasoning):
  1. The detective is a genius with tremendous deductive thinking abilities.
  2. The actions and abilities of the detective mystify the narrator of the story. (Therefore, his stories are written in the first person point of view.)
  3. Nothing should be hidden from the reader, but the secret of the mystery must not be revealed.
  4. The story must evolve around the clues and how the detective uses his intellect to decipher the clues and solve the crime.

- Students will research the mysteries of other disciplines independently.

Product

- Students will create clues of a mystery story for another group of students to solve.
- Students will write and perform a mystery play.
- Students will generate questions and participate in a student-run seminar.

II. The Lesson

◆ **Motivation**

1. Students "Create a Crime."
   - Ask students to identify the features of a detective story (crime, detectives, suspects, clues, and suspense).
   - Divide students into two groups. The groups can be within one class or two separate classes.
   - Tell the students they are going to create a crime. Swear them to secrecy.
   - Explain to the students that they are to decide on a crime and then create the clues that would help a detective solve the crime. (The teacher might want to place limitations on this so that they don't choose something inappropriate for their age.)
     — The clues can be pictures, items they create or bring from home, riddles, etc.
     — They must include all the clues and suspects that are needed to solve the crime.
     — They may include red herrings (suspects or clues that are distractors).
     — They will put all of the clues in a grocery bag or some other type of container (maybe even something that is a clue).
     — They will give the teacher a written, chronological, logical scenario of their crime and the solution.
   - Have students trade their evidence bags with the other group/class. They will become detectives themselves and use inductive logic to piece together the clues from the other group and decide what the crime is and solve the mystery.
2. Discussion:
   - Ask the students what difficulties they encountered. If students were unable to solve the crime or decipher the clues, relate this to real detective work or to the work that a scientist does.
   - Ask them what other disciplines/jobs require this type of inductive logic and problem-solving skills (scientific and historical research, accounting, mathematical and statistical studies, archaeology, space exploration).
   - Ask them how and when people use logic and "detective" skills in their daily lives.

Teacher Notes Con't

- Current definition of a detective story:
  1. The story should appeal to the reader's sense of justice (good should triumph over evil). (Theme)
  2. The detective is a hero because of his or her powers of reasoning and logic. (Character)
  3. The story must be suspenseful. (Mood/tone)
  4. The clues necessary to solve the crime are presented to help the reader/viewer solve the mystery. Some of the clues can be red herrings to throw suspicion off the real culprit. (Rising action)
  5. There must be a crime. (Conflict)

3. Optional Reading—Select a detective story and delete the solution (Agatha Christie's "The Tape Measure Murder" or a Miss Marple story work well).
   - Ask the students to read the story and predict the outcome (who committed the crime and his or her motive).
   - Ask students to explain the inductive and deductive logical thinking they used to arrive at the solution.
   - Authenticate the students' answers by reading the end of the story describing the solution of the crime.

◆ Input

Poe/Doyle/Christie Short Story and Novel Study and Seminar

1. Provide the students background on the genre and noted authors of the genre (see Independent Research/Interdisciplinary Studies #1). Tell students that Poe is the father of the detective story or what he called "tales of ratiocination."

2. Have the students look up *ratiocination* and find its etymological basis. Discuss whether this term is more appropriate than "detective/mystery" story. [L. *ratio-cinat-*reckoned, calculated, concluded; derived from *ratio* – reason].

3. Assign one short story by Poe, one by Doyle, and then a novel (or short story) by Christie in order to see both the changes and what has remained consistent in the detective genre.
   - Edgar Allan Poe—"Murders in the Rue Morgue" or "Purloined Letter"—These are somewhat challenging until students become used to Poe's style, so the teacher might want to begin reading these stories in class or summarize the first few paragraphs wherein Poe establishes the story and then have students read the rest of the story on their own.
   - Sir Arthur Conan Doyle—"Red Headed League," "The Speckled Band," "Adventures of the Blue Carbuncle," or "The Dying Detective"
   - Agatha Christie—*Murder on the Orient Express* or *And Then There Were None* (*Ten Little Indians*)

Student Seminar

1. Explain to the class how college seminars operate. Distribute the Student Seminar Study Starter to the students. Review the expectations related to completing the worksheet.

2. Tell the students that they will be participating in a discussion-based seminar to discuss the short stories and novel the class reads. Explain that they will not only be focusing on the characters and plots, but also on the detective genre. Ask them to pay special attention to the relationships within each story (how characters and their relationships cause conflict) and also to the patterns and relationships between and among the stories they read.

3. Tell the students that each of them is responsible for generating a set of discussion questions. These questions are to be open-ended and allow for discussion and disagreement. For example:
   - Why did Character A _____?
   - How do you think Character B felt about _____?
   - What would you have done if you had been in Character C's situation?
   - Why did the author _____?
   - What relationships do you see between _____ and _____?

4. Conduct the seminar by setting up the classroom with two circles of desks, one inside the other. Establish the following criteria with the students:
   - The students in the outer circle will ask the questions and are responsible for keeping the discussion moving. These students may not respond to questions unless they challenge an answer by asking another question.
   - The students in the inside circle will respond to the questions. They may use their books to quote passages and locate information as needed.
   - Students will participate without raising their hands. They must be polite to each other—no interruptions.
   - Students may add to other people's responses, but repetition is discouraged.
   - They must allow and encourage everyone to participate, and they should not dominate the discussion.
   - The teacher will guide as needed, but this will be done minimally.
   - Halfway through the discussion period, the students will switch circles and continue the discussion.

Teacher-Directed Class Discussion

1. Ask students what relationships they see between Dupin and modern detectives in movies or on television. What traits does a good detective have (observation skills, good people skills, power of reasoning, understanding of human nature, imagination, and so forth)?
2. Compare/contrast Dupin to Sherlock Holmes and Hercule Poirot and to other detectives on television.
3. Discuss the relationships the various detective stories have in common (characters, plot, theme, style, etc.)
4. Ask these questions:
   - What types of relationships do the characters in the stories have with other characters?
   - Are these relationships/conflicts the same across all or most mystery/detective stories?
   - What aspects of the detective/mystery genre have stayed the same over time? Why is this so?
   - How has the genre (pattern) changed and why have these changes evolved?
   - What changes do you think will take place in the genre in the future? Why?

Teacher Notes

If you wish to grade students on their discussion, create a blank class roster. Give students points for creating quality questions. As the discussion takes place, give students a plus (+) for an insightful or higher level thinking response, a check (✓) for adding a relevant comment, and a minus (–) for interrupting or arguing. Having this chart will allow you to see the patterns in the discussion and guide students who have not participated or who have dominated the discussion. You can then give them a grade for their participation.

Optional Activities

1. Encourage students to read "The Adventure of the Final Problem" on their own. (Sherlock Holmes dies in this story.) Have them write the story Doyle might have written to bring Holmes "back from the dead."

2. Introduce Code Breaking—Have students read or view Poe's "The Gold Bug." The story is somewhat tedious, so find an adapted or simplified version. *Read* magazine, February 19, 1988, has a play version, and Coronet Film & Video made a film version.
   - Discuss why reviewers don't feel this is a true detective story.
   - Hand out Code Breaking—Study Starter to the students.
   - Have students decode the sentence. If they become stuck, give them a second letter pair (X = I).
   - The answer to the code is "If you can break this code, you can create a code and send secret messages to your friends."
   - This is the substitution key used:
   - A B C D E F G H I J K L M N O P Q R S T U V W X Y Z equals
   - B L T C O Z E F X R N A J U D V P G Q M K S Y W I H

3. Have students draw names for a "secret code pal" and have them exchange messages using their own substitution code.

◆ **Output**

Students will write and perform a detective play with an altered pattern.

1. Ask students to brainstorm possible characters (including criminals and detectives), crimes, settings, and clues.
   - Create lists of names of potential detectives/characters in a mystery. These can be detectives or characters in stories or movies, or students can create original characters.
   - List possible crimes for the characters.
   - List unusual items that could be clues—don't accept the ordinary!
   - List possible settings for the stories.

2. Write each idea on a colored note card. Categorize them topically by using one color (e.g., blue) for characters, one color (e.g., green) for crimes, and so forth.

3. Ask students to brainstorm and create a list of terms that relate to the discipline of criminal investigation using the chart below:

Crimes/Legal Terminology	Investigative Techniques	Detectives/Law Enforcement Personnel	Criminals

4. Divide students into groups of four or five.

5. Have each group select two character cards, a crime card, two clue cards, and a setting card. These must be included in their story; however, they may add more characters,

clues, and so forth.

6. Hand out the "Mystery, We Write" Study Starter to help them with their brainstorming.

7. Explain to the students that they must make one change or adaptation to the pattern/features of the detective genre. (Use the SCAMPER strategy: Substitute, Combine, Adapt, Modify, Put to other uses, Eliminate, Rearrange. For example, students may make the detective a bungling character, they may make the theme "crime does pay," or they may make the criminal a hero.)

8. Tell students that they must use the language or terminology of the discipline. Tell them to use some of the terms they listed in their charts.

Teacher Notes

(Possible terminology of the discipline)
- **Crimes and legal terminology**—manslaughter, homicide, larceny, libel, slander, counterfeiting, burglary, robbery, felony, arson, extortion, misdemeanor, grand theft, first and second degree murder, white collar crime, civil court, criminal court, grand jury, habeas corpus, assault, preliminary hearing, plea bargain, arrest warrant, perjury, corpus delicti, acquit, convict, guilt, innocence.
- **Investigative techniques**—forensic medicine, modus operandi, tail, paraphernalia, DNA testing, wiretapping, stakeouts, lie detectors, autopsy, bugs, lineup, whorls/loops/arches in fingerprints, APB, surveillance, computerized age progression, ballistics.
- **Detectives/law enforcement personnel**—gumshoe, private detective, sheriff, bailiff, bail bondsman, prosecutor, defending attorney, policeman, judge.
- **Criminals**—crook, hoodlum, villain, felon, culprit, forger, blackmailer, hooligan, thief, pilferer, kleptomaniac, purloiner, second story man, shoplifter, swindler, accomplice.

9. Review how a play is formatted so that their scripts are appropriate for the discipline. (Have students open their literature book to a drama to let them identify the details of the style/format.)

10. Have the students perform their plays for the class (or for other classes). Suggestion: videotape the performances.

Detective Play Evaluation/Assessment

Students will be graded on:
- following the pattern of a detective story (one exception is allowed), using the characters, crime, clues, and settings they drew from the card sets;
- staying within the allotted time;
- creativity of script, costumes, props;
- using play format, correct spelling, and grammar; and
- performance (including memorization of lines and using rate, volume, pitch, and tone appropriate for the dialogue).

◆ Culmination
Class Discussion

1. Prepare students to assume the role of discussion participants. Use these questions to stimulate ideas.
   - What generalizations can be made about mysteries?

> # Teacher Notes
>
> The pattern of the typical short story or novel is broken because the climax (the crime) takes place at the beginning. This becomes the complication of the detective story, and the detective has to piece together the events that led to the crime.

   - Ask students why mysteries are so popular. What is the appeal?
   - Discuss why some criminals have become heroes (Robin Hood, Jesse James, Billy the Kid).
   - Why do crime and criminals fascinate people? (O. J. Simpson, Lizzie Borden, Lee Harvey Oswald, Sacco and Vanzetti, Jack the Ripper, the Boston Strangler, Charles Manson, and so forth.)
   - Why does the plot design/pattern of a detective story not follow a typical short story? Have students figure out why the plot design is different.

2. Discuss crime in the United States.
   - What is the relationship of crime to movies, television, and music?
   - Are we becoming more violent?
   - What causes violence and crime?
   - What should be done about it?
   - At what age should people be held responsible for their behavior?
   - Should parents be liable for crimes their children commit?

Additional reading of the genre

Encourage students to read modern detective novels by authors such as Tom Clancy, Sue Grafton, and so forth. Have students conduct book talks with the teacher or set up literature circles or book groups and let them discuss the books among themselves.

◆ Extensions
—Independent Research Topics
—Interdisciplinary Options

Allow students to define their own topics. The following are some ideas:

1. Research significant authors of the detective genre.
   - Research Poe, Doyle, or Christie and make a presentation before the class reads the stories.
   - Research and evaluate several authors and/or detective stories. Choose which should be included in a Mystery Hall of Fame. Be sure to include the criteria upon which the decision is made.
   - Read and analyze several mystery short stories by various authors. What relationships can be found among them in terms of style or treatment of the genre?

2. Consider topics relating to crime and law enforcement.
   - Research crime statistics and note the patterns and trends. Based on these relationships, predict what types of crime will be more predominant in the future.
   - Research a famous crime and conduct a mock trial of the case.
   - Research modern techniques used to solve crimes, such as DNA testing and age advancement done by computers, the use of television in finding criminals, and so forth.
   - Research the roles of law enforcement agencies (at least four) of various times and places. Create a brochure that compares and contrasts these organizations (FBI, CIA, KGB, Scotland Yard, Canadian Mounted Police, local police departments, sheriff's department, private detectives, Pinkerton Agency, sheriffs in the Middle Ages, sheriffs on the American frontier, etc.).
   - Research code breaking—history of, uses in World War II, genetic code breaking, codes being used to "talk" to other beings in space. (Relate this to the movie *Contact* and how three-dimensional thinking broke the code.)

3. Research the mysteries of math on topics such as:
   - the discovery of *pi* (an irrational number) in numerous cultures centuries apart and how this relationship is used in architecture;
   - the mysteries of the number 8 (chess, music, etc.);
   - exponential growth (have them figure out how much allowance they would make in one month if they start with one penny at the beginning of the month and double their allowance each day—it goes to the millions); and
   - chaos theory (remind them of *Jurassic Park*), Pascal's triangle, mobius strip, imaginary numbers such as the square root of negative one, fractals—patterns in math (take a shape and create a design), Fibonacci theory of math in nature (pine cones, sea shells, etc.).

4. Research the mysteries of science/history on topics such as:
   - pyramids;
   - statues on Easter Island;
   - Stonehenge;
   - Bermuda Triangle;
   - Atlantis;
   - black holes;
   - quarks;
   - quasars;
   - Big Bang Theory; and
   - individuality of snowflakes and fingerprints.

—Classical Connections
- Mock trial—put a character from one of the detective stories on trial.
- Invite a lawyer or judge to discuss the legal system in class.
- Debate issues relating to crime and the legal system.
- Visit a hands-on science museum.

—Philosophy

To make sense of a sometimes mysterious world, Aristotle challenged his students with a kind of problem called a *syllogism*. The syllogism has three parts, each worded in a particular way. The first line gives a piece of information, and the second line gives another piece of information. These statements are called *premises*. These premises are combined to form the conclusion, the third statement.

> *Example:*
> All men are mortal.
> Socrates is a man.
> Therefore, Socrates is mortal.

Syllogisms may be valid (true) or invalid (not true), depending on whether the conclusion is supported by the premises or not. Introduce students to this form of logical reasoning as a means for getting at the truth. Sources for teaching logic and syllogisms include Dean Crawford's *Logic Countdown* and *Orbiting With Logic* (Dandy Lion Publications) and *Logic, Anyone?* by Post and Eads (Fearon Teacher Aids).

—Adaptations for Other Grade Levels

- Elementary—This unit can be adapted by using simplified, adapted versions of Poe's and Doyle's stories and using detective novels for younger audiences.
  — Introduce *The Man Who Was Poe* by Avi. This is an excellent book because Poe is the detective in the story. Give the students background on Poe so that they see the relationships.
  — *Mysteries of Harris Burdick* or *The Westing Game* are good choices, as well.
  — Read *Motel of the Mysteries*. Have the students become archeologists of the 30th century. They have just discovered the remains of a wondrous site—this school. As 30th-century archeologists, they must interpret the artifacts they find. They must draw pictures and label the artifacts and their surmised uses.

Student Seminar

I. You will be participating in a discussion-based seminar. You will discuss the short stories and novel the class reads. You will not only be focusing on the characters and plots, but also on the detective genre. To prepare for the discussion, you will need to generate a set of discussion questions. These questions are to be open-ended and allow for discussion and disagreement and should allow for factual, analytic, and valuative responses. The following question patterns might help you generate your own:

   A. Why did Character A do _____?
   B. How do you think Character B felt about _____?
   C. What would you have done if you had been in Character C's situation?
   D. Why did the author _____?
   E. What relationships do you see between _____ and _____?

II. On the day of the discussion, the classroom will be set up with two circles of desks, one inside the other.

   A. Outer Circle's responsibilities:
   This will be like being a host or hostess at a dinner party. The host/hostess is responsible for keeping the discussion lively and shifting topics when the discussion dies out.

   1. The students in the outer circle will ask the questions and are responsible for keeping the discussion moving.
   2. These students may not respond to questions unless they challenge an answer by asking another question.

   B. Inner Circle's responsibilities:
   You are the gracious guest.

   1. The students in the inside circle will respond to the questions.
   2. You may use your books to quote passages and locate information as needed.
   3. No hands will be raised.
   4. You must be polite to each other—no interruptions or arguing. You may disagree politely.
   5. Students may add to other people's responses, but repetition is discouraged.
   6. Students must allow and encourage everyone to participate and not dominate the discussion.

   Halfway through the discussion period, students will switch circles and continue the discussion.

III. Assessment: You will be graded on the quality of your questions and answers, as well as for following the established guidelines of the discussion as given above.

Mysteries, We Write!

You and the members of your group will write a play that will be the pilot for a weekly television show. In creating your drama, you will follow the basic pattern of a detective story, **but you will break one rule to change that pattern**. Use proper drama (play) format.

Crime _____

Setting _____

Detective(s) _____ _____

Suspects _____ _____

_____ _____

Clues _____ _____

_____ _____

Sound Effect(s) _____ _____

Which rule/feature of a detective story are you changing?_____

_____

Professional Detective Terminology (terminology of the discipline)

_____ _____

_____ _____

_____ _____

- You will have 20 minutes to present your play. (Ten minutes of a 30 minute show will be commercials). You will have four minutes to set up and four to clean up.
- You must include costumes and props.
- Each member of the group must have a significant role in the performance.
- Lines must be memorized and spoken with appropriate expression—inflection, volume, and pitch.
- Provide the teacher with a copy of the script. Highlight the terminology of the discipline.
- Be sure you have applied the conventions of grammar, punctuation, and spelling.

Detective Play Evaluation/Assessment

You will be graded on:
- using characters, crime, clues, and settings on the cards with **one exception**;
- staying within the allotted time;
- creativity of script, costumes, and props;
- using play format, correct spelling, and grammar; and
- performance (including memorization of lines and using rate, volume, pitch, and tone appropriate for the dialogue).

Code Breaking

Use the substitution method of code breaking to decipher the following message. Think of the patterns of phonics in the English language and the relationship of sequence of letters and which letters are used most often to help you. Q = S

XZ IDK TBU LGOBN MFXQ TDCO IDK TBU TGOBMO B

__ ___ ___ _____ ____ ____ ___ ___ _____ _

TDCO BUC QOUC QOTGOM JOQQBEOQ

____ ___ ____ _____ _____

MD IDKG ZGXOUCQ

__ ____ _____

As you figure out the pattern, write the letter substitutions in the blanks below the letters.

A B C D E F G H I J K L M N O P Q R S T U V W X Y Z

_ _

Mysterious Illusions: Op Art

Art can be deliberately mysterious and startling.

Op Art is a style of art that was developed in the United States in the '60s. The subject matter of these paintings was nonobjective. The artists were not interested in painting something that looked like a recognizable object. Instead, they created paintings using lines and shapes that they organized into designs that seemed to create a sense of movement, depth, or other effects. Op artists created these deceptions of visual perception on either flat canvas or flat paper. The artists often used very limited palettes, two to six hues. Many Op Art compositions were limited to just two colors, black and white. Two important artists of the Op Art art movement are Victor Vasarely and Bridget Riley.

Objective

The students will create a black-and-white Op Art design that creates either an illusion of movement or depth on a flat surface.

Materials

- art history books and art textbooks
- design books
- Internet research
- 9" x 9" newsprint (preliminary sketch)
- 9" x 9" white drawing paper
- pencil
- eraser
- fine-point felt-tipped pen
- compass, ruler

Procedure for the Illusion of Movement

1. Practice drawing wavy lines that are parallel to each other.
2. If the lines are placed close to each other, you will notice a sense of movement.
3. Practice drawing concentric circles using a compass. You might need to place a piece of poster board or heavy paper under the practice paper to keep the point of the compass stationary.
4. The spacing of the concentric circles can be constant or change gradually. Gradual changes in the spacing will create illusions of depth.
5. Once the desired effect is achieved on the practice paper, draw the desired composition on the white drawing paper in pencil.
6. Trace the pencil lines with a fine-point felt-tipped marker.

Procedure for the Illusion of Depth

1. Find the center of the square sheet of white paper by drawing a diagonal line from one corner to the opposite corner of the square.
2. The intersection of the two lines is the center of the square.
3. Starting at the center of the square and using a ruler, make a mark at every ½" along each diagonal line starting at the center of the square.
4. Align a ruler along one side of the square and mark every ½" to 1". Whichever dimension you select, it must be constant around the perimeter of the square.
5. Do this to each side of the square. Now draw a straight line using the ruler connecting the mark on one side through the center point of the square to the mark on the opposite side of the square.
6. Now that all of the lines are drawn, the result should be a design of concentric squares with straight lines radiating from the center of the squares.
7. To complete the design, trace the lines with a fine-point felt-tipped pen and color in the small shapes, alternating black with the white paper to create a checker-like pattern.
8. The finished product will give the viewer a sense of depth. The space of the pattern will appear to recess in the center of the squares.

Evaluation

Did the student create an optical illusion?

Art Reference Books

The Art Book. (1998.) London: Phaidon.

Janson, H. W. (1997). *The history of art.* New York: H. Abrams.

Strickland, C. & Boswell, J. (1992). *The annotated Mona Lisa: A crash course in art history from prehistoric to postmodern.* Kansas City: Andrews & McNeel.

Tansey, R. (1995). *Gardner's Art Through the Ages.* New York: HBJ.

Illusion of Depth

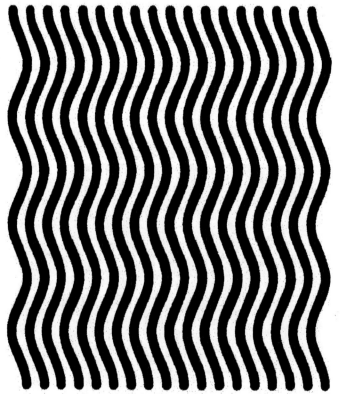

Illusion of Movement

Diversity: A Unifying Force

I. Teacher Preparation

◆ **Background**
Time Required: 3 weeks

Getting Ready
For this lesson you will need the following:
- bag of trash;
- rubber gloves;
- old newspapers;
- current newspapers;
- egg timer;
- small spiral or composition book; and
- state/area map.

Curriculum Standards

The student will:

Primary Standard
- Explain how cultural diversity is reflected in language, celebrations, and performances.

Embedded Content and Skills
- Pose and answer questions about geographic distributions and patterns.
- Trace development of major industries.
- Describe the importance of free speech and press and defend a point of view.
- Evaluate the effects of scientific discoveries.

Curriculum Standard Level:
Introductory X   Developmental   Extension

◆ Framework

Theme: Relationships

Generalization: Diverse cultural, physical, and economic regions create relationships that either unify or isolate them as a larger geographic area (within political boundaries), as well as with other regions of the world.

Content Focus: The cultural diversity in a city or state contributes to the images of the place and people.

Rationale: Through independent investigation of assigned towns or cities, students will understand how cultural diversity has been and still is an important aspect of society.

Differentiation Framework

Thinking Skills	Depth/Complexity	Research	Products
• Identify relationships • Identify charac-teristics/attributes • Hypothesize	• Details • Patterns	• Locate and analyze online newspapers	• Radio broadcast reflecting regional cultures

Thinking Skills

- **Relationships**—to identify how two or more items are linked or connected.
  Example: Students will explain the connection between geographic locations and food consumption/production.
- **Identify characteristics/attributes**—to describe traits that make things unique.
  Example: Students will relate unique cultural traits specific to a variety of regions.
- **Think inductively**—to define a number of observations and draw a conclusion from them.
  Example: Students define elements of a regional newspaper and make conclusions about cultural traits along with cultural origins of the people of the region.
- **Hypothesize**—to make an assumption based on collected information.
  Example: Students draw a hypothesis of the relationship between two different regions.

Depth/Complexity

- **Details**—the parts, attributes, factors, or variables inherent to the whole.
  Example: Students will identify the details or attributes of the four geographic regions.
- **Patterns**—Reoccurring events or related events that are predictable and repetitive.
  Example: Students will describe patterns (including economic, religious, and social) found within a particular region and across all regions of an area.

Research

- **Conduct online research**—to conduct online analysis of newspapers from selected geographic regions.

  Example: Students will create charts to record information found in newspapers and to define the details and cultural patterns of a geographic region.

Product

- **Produce a radio broadcast**—to assume the role of a radio broadcaster who generates a program based on evidence gathered from news events and lifestyle trends from a given cultural region.

  Example: Students will produce a news broadcast that reflects the uniqueness of a cultural region.

II. The Lesson

◆ Motivation

1. Divide students into heterogeneous cooperative groups with four students per group. Each group will need a leader, scribe, timekeeper, and resource person (gathers, distributes, or returns materials).
2. Distribute one pair of rubber gloves and a large piece of newspaper to each group.
3. Empty a bag of trash onto a desk or table at the front of the classroom.
4. Tell students they are about to become anthropologists—scientists who analyze and classify the systems that humans have created to help them control or give structure to their lives. Have students brainstorm a list of the systems they believe humans have created to give structure to their lives. Record responses for the class. (Responses should include language, religion, government, economic systems, rites of passage, play, work, social and family organization, marriage, arts, food and food production, customs, habits, and so forth.) Tell students that these systems reflect cultural traits. Next, explain that the job of the anthropologist is to define the details, patterns, and relationships between and among objects in order to identify and explain the traits that make each cultural group distinct.
5. Ask the resource person from each group to come and take some of the trash from the pile and place it on a newspaper at his or her desk.
6. Give students the following instructions:

   "Examine the trash that has been placed with your group. Only the resource person may actually pick up or handle the items. You will have five minutes to analyze the trash and discuss your discoveries with your group. When the timer sounds, your group will move clockwise to the next group's trash pile and again examine the trash. This procedure will continue until you have had an opportunity to examine each group's trash. Carefully examine the trash at each desk; let no detail go unnoticed. Scribes will record their group's findings and conclusions on the Study Starter."
7. Students may record information on the following chart in order to define and discuss their findings from the trash piles.

Patterns	Items That Belong Together	Location	Relationship of Items to each other/to the environment

8. Have the groups orally present their findings to the class. Discuss what students have identified that they believe to be the cultural traits of the people who left the trash behind. Finally, as a class, create a summary statement describing the culture based on the findings from the trash.

◆ **Input**

1. Tell students that they will be using their examination of knowledge and experiences, along with skills used by anthropologists and other academicians, in order to make some generalizations about the diversity (variety) of cultures across the area. These generalizations will serve as reference and focal points for the study of the rich history and cultural heritage.

2. Instruct students to use symbols of the state to label and decorate the front of small spiral or composition notebooks to use as journals.

3. Introduce students to the different roles of academicians such as philosopher, anthropologist, and sociologist. Discuss the importance of the language of the disciplines for use with the academicians. Have students assume the role of an academician when they record their findings, feelings, and impressions in their journals.

4. Review the details or characteristics of a region with the class.
   - *A region is an area that has one or more features throughout its boundaries that sets it apart. The features may be political, economic, cultural, or physical.*
   - Have students locate and identify different geographic regions of the state or area. Students then will record hypotheses about the relationship between the physical features of the geography and the economic, political, and cultural lifestyles of the people within the region. Ask students: In what ways does lifestyle mirror environment? Relate the answer to the question to a particular area or region. Ask students to do the same task independently.

   ## Teacher Note

   Due to its size, history as a separate nation, and diversity of cultures, Texas has been referred to as a virtual nation-state within a nation. It shares both geographical and cultural characteristics with other regions of the world.

5. Have students respond to the following question in their journals:
   - *Why do you hypothesize that geography has had a significant impact on both the history and the present-day development of the state or region?*
   - Have students share their responses. Develop a collage of written responses to illustrate both responses and regional diversity.

6. Define culture as a way of life; the pattern of people's knowledge, skills, and beliefs. These patterns of knowledge, skills, and beliefs are cultural traits. Define ethnic groups as people who share a common racial, national, religious, or cultural background. Have students describe their own ethnic backgrounds. Also have them describe the cultural characteristics of their region in their journals. Ask for volunteers to share their journal responses with the class. Discuss the possible differences in the students' perceptions of cultural regions.

7. Have students explain, from the point of view of their disciplinarian or academician, the relationship between ethnic and cultural groups. Respond to the following questions when explaining their point of view:
    *   How do these groups interact?
    *   Is it possible for a cultural group to have members of several ethnic groups?
    *   Do all ethnic groups share the same religion?

8. Working with their groups, have students list different ethnic groups that live in the city/region. (Allow students five minutes for brainstorming.) Have students share their lists and combine them into one.

9. Ask students to respond to the following statement:
    *   *This region is diverse in both size and cultural ethnic groups. Yet, even with this diversity, there exists preconceived notions about the stereotypical Texan.*

10. In their groups, have students brainstorm the traits of a typical citizen of the city/region. Once students have brainstormed these traits, have them share with the class.

11. Ask students if these traits are the same for people who live in all cultural regions of the state. Be sure to have students elaborate upon their responses.

12. Instruct students to respond to the truism, "Our city/region is a state of mind," in their journals.

◆ **Output**

1. Place students into cooperative groups. Give each group a complete newspaper, which will be used as a reference to describe the features of a newspaper. Ask students to examine their newspaper and to discuss its format, categories of information found within it, and the types of writing used in the publication. Be sure to have scribes write the groups' discoveries about the newspapers on a piece of paper. Groups should share responses with the entire class.

Teacher Note

Be sure to point out that newspapers are organized to meet a variety of needs. Papers contain news stories that give updates of current events. News stories usually contain a headline that catches the reader's attention, a byline that names the person who reported the event, a dateline that tells where the event took place, and the information explaining the event. Papers employ both news-writing and feature-writing techniques. These are sections that deal with leisure time and entertainment, the business world, sports, or are just for fun reading.

2. Tell students that they will be researching a city or town by using the Internet to view online newspapers. As anthropologists and sociologists use clues, actions, and behaviors

to understand and identify the cultural traits of a group of people, students will use these online newspapers as clues to identify the cultural traits of the regions to which they are assigned. If the class has access to only one computer with an Internet connection, each group will have to take turns on the computer. If

Teacher Note

Go to the Internet site **http://www.newsdirectory.com/news/press/na/us/** and search through the list of both daily and nondaily papers. Newspapers are organized according to area codes. It is suggested that you assign groups community papers from a variety of zip codes, both small and large communities, daily papers, and nondaily papers.

that is the case, it is suggested that the groups print hard copies of as much of the information found on their site as possible to save time.

3. Inform students that each cooperative group will now act as a team of anthropologists who are working together to identify cultural traits of a community.

4. Assign each group a community newspaper to read, discuss, and analyze. Instruct students to follow these steps in order to complete their assignment:

   - Use your anthropological journals to keep a detailed record of your investigations and analysis.
   - Log on to the Internet. Go to http://www.newsdirectory.com/news/press/na/us/.
   - Find the title of the newspaper you have been assigned. Look at the names of the cities and towns that are grouped with your newspaper. Locate the surrounding communities on a map. Record what you can assume about the physical region in which your newspaper is located.
   - Read and explore the entire newspaper site. Use what you have found about this region to make generalizations about cultural traits of this community. Define the categories and create an advanced organizer to complete while investigating the regional newspaper online: language, religion, government, economic system, rites of passage, play or leisure, work, social and family organization, marriage, the arts, food, shelter, beliefs, and customs.
   - Record your findings under the category that best fits the information. Summarize the research you have collected by describing patterns and trends.
   - Use the completed information from your investigation of the online site to summarize your hypotheses of the cultural traits of the community represented by your newspaper. Include in the hypotheses the relationship of this community to other communities and regions not only within the state, but also outside the state or region. Use the Internet for additional research. Describe as many traits of the culture of the community as you can.

5. Once each group has drawn a hypothesis, assign the next phase of the assignment.

   - Using the information you have gathered, you will be writing and producing a 10-minute local radio program to air in the community you studied. The program must reflect the cultural traits of the community and must be of value or importance to that community. The broadcast must include a brief local news break and at least two commercials that reflect unique products or services for the community. Broadcasts will be aired live from our classroom studios. Be sure to use the "On the Air" Study Starter as a guide to complete the assignment.

Teacher Note

This activity can be used as an interdisciplinary lesson with a language arts class. Language arts connections include writing dialogue for scripts, the relationship between the written and spoken word, and using propaganda techniques for advertising.

5. Arrange the classroom so that radio programs may be performed in such a way that students cannot see the performances; they should only be able to hear them. This can be done by either staging the performances behind the other students (the listeners' backs to the performers) or by hanging sheets across the front of the classroom.

6. Before each group airs its program, have them point to the location of the community being represented on a map.

7. Remind students that these programs represent regions throughout the state. Focus students' attention on several aspects of the programs, including types of programs aired, products represented through the commercials, geographic location, and local news breaks. As the programs progress, students are responsible for identifying specific cultural traits for the community, the relationship of each community with other communities across or outside of the state, and traits (characteristics) that seem to be common to many of the communities.

8. Generate a class discussion by asking the following questions:
   - Who are some of the different ethnic groups represented in the programs?
   - What do many of the radio programs have in common?
   - What relationships do these communities have with each other?
   - How do settlement patterns, trends, and environmental relationships contribute to form the culture of each region?
   - How do the relationships of diverse cultural traditions provide unity?
   - What is a "_____ citizen?" What makes this person different from citizens of other states?

◆ Culmination

Describe and show examples of photojournalistic essays to students. Define the attributes of communicating in the medium. Explain to students that they will be creating a photojournalistic document about their community. Use disposable or digital cameras to develop a photojournalistic essay of the city or region or to portray the economic, social, political, academic, and so forth, diversity within the area. Organize an exhibition with questions about trends and patterns posted along with the essays to guide observations and evoke communication.

◆ Extensions
—Independent Research Topics

1. Research population changes in the state from 1900 to 1960 to today. Find out about the distribution of minorities by counties or regions, both rural and urban. Create three

maps that illustrate the diversity of the changes in population. Describe within a given time period how these population distributions have changed. Identify the reasons for these changes. Predict future population trends. Explain your predictions and the evidence on which the predictions were based.

2. Discuss the idea that the big screen has always had an important relationship with a state or region. Research the movie industry's use of specific geographic areas in films. Use a movie you have researched in order to identify and correct the geographical inaccuracies or create a storyboard for a movie to be filmed in your community. Write a proposal to a producer that includes the storyboard and the benefits of filming in your community.

3. Introduce the concept that state regional politics have been marked by its heroes and marred by the corrupt. The U.S. Senator Joe Bailey once vowed to bury his enemies "face down so that the harder they scratch to get out, the deeper they go." Research personalities of state or regional politics. Choose several you would consider to be heroes and several you would consider corrupt. Create a book, *Political Heroes and Zeros of Our State*. For each, draw a portrait, write a brief biographical sketch, and describe his or her political impact and its effect across the state. Bind the information together as a book with a final chapter (section) that defines and describes the effects of politicians on the diverse cultural groups of the state.

4. Research different influences on music in the state/region. Learn about a personality in the history of music, especially local figures. Put on a television show, *This is Your Life*, highlighting the personality's life and accomplishments in music. Be sure to include music in the show.

—Literary Connections

Read selections of a regional writer, such as O. Henry in Texas, and identify the cultural influences in his writing.

—Classical Connections: Philosophy

The ancient Greek philosopher Protagoras believed that truth was relative—it depended on the situation, place, and time—and he rejected the idea of absolute truth on any subject. He is reputed to have said "Man is the measure of all things." Discuss this quote and the idea of knowing what is true with the students. Have groups write statements that are always true about how people should act. As a class, list different regions or ethnic or racial groups. How would each region or ethnic or racial group respond to the list of "true" statements? Are there any statements that all groups would acknowledge? What statements would have the most disagreements?

Trash Investigations

You are now anthropologists. It is your task to examine the items contained in the trash bag to draw some conclusions about the people who left the trash behind. Complete the sheet with your group as you discuss and analyze the clues.

Items and how were they were used: _____

_____

Items that are related: _____

_____

Patterns of objects or patterns of use: _____

_____

Physical location of the people: _____

_____

Hypotheses:
Describe the cultural traits of the people:_____

_____

(Remember, cultural traits may include language, religion, government, economic systems, rites of passage, play, work, social and family organization, marriage, the arts, food and food productions, customs, habits, and so forth.)

On the Air

The following steps will help you produce and air your radio show. Use your journal to take notes, respond to each step, and organize your tasks.

Step One: Plan the Program

- **Simulate a market analysis** of the viewing community. Use the cultural traits and hypotheses you have drawn from the online newspaper to determine viewer interests for local programming. Your market analysis will answer some, but not be limited to, the following questions:
    — Which physical (geographic) regions will air the program?
    — What are some cultural traits of the community that make it unique?
    — How do people make a living? What do people do during their leisure time?
    — What is the predominant religion? What is the size of the community?
    — What type of food is consumed? How do people express themselves artistically (music, visual arts, drama)?
- **Consider the market** (listening audience) in order to determine …
    — the time of day the program will air.
    — the day of the week the program will air.
    — the average age of the target audience.
    — the relationship of this community with other counties, states, or countries.
- **Choose the program format** that will be best suited for the target audience. Suggestions for formats:
    — a morning talk show
    — a variety show
    — a locally created drama
    — a political debate regarding local issues
    — coverage of a local event
    — an infomercial from the local chamber of commerce
- **Decide who will be the sponsors** of the program.
    Sponsors will advertise local products or services.

Step Two: Produce the Radio Program

- **Write a script for the program** that includes:
    — the program introduction (must be clever and catchy);
    — commercial breaks (both timing and scripts);
    — who will speak and the manner in which it will be delivered (consider pacing; vocal inflections; purpose, such as to inform, entertain, or convince); and
    — at least one local news break.

- **Add the professional touches.** After all, a radio broadcast relies solely on the listener's ability to translate what he or she hears into a visual picture.
  — Add sound effects and music to bring the production to life.

- **Practice the broadcast** and fine tune it so that the debut is of professional quality. Be sure to work on timings, vocal quality, transitions (such as to and from commercial breaks), and so forth.
  — Practice with an audience (ask them to keep their backs to you).

- **Air/perform the broadcast.**
  — Have fun! Perform with enthusiasm.

Native American Pictographs

Ancient pictographs add another element to the diversity.

Thousands of years ago, prehistoric people lived on this land that we know as the United States. Evidence of their existence was left behind in extraordinary pictographs and petroglyphs. These images were created on the walls of rocks and rock shelters throughout several states. Many of these historic treasures are protected by state and federal laws. Pictographs are scattered throughout the states and are among the most impressive treasures of Native American art in the country. Historians and archeologists study the images to give us insight into the cultures of prehistoric people. The truth is that they will never truly realize what many of the images represent.

In Europe, this is especially true of the prehistoric cave paintings of Lascaux, France, and Altamira, Spain. Historians and archeologists can only hypothesize the significance of the images represented in these magnificent works of art. We assume that the stylized images created by prehistoric people are recordings of important events in their lives. The prehistoric art of the aborigines of Australia is as important to their culture today as it was thousands of years ago. The beliefs of the aborigines of Australia have been carefully preserved through painted images that represent "the dreaming" or the stories of the creation.

Objective

The students will explore the prehistoric pictographs and petroglyphs by creating a timeline of the images represented in these forms of art. The students will hypothesize the meanings of the images.

Materials

- Videos and books of Native American rock art
- other state and National Park resources
- craft paper 36" x 10'
- pencils
- erasers
- ruled paper for note taking
- colored chalk
- aerosol hair spray

Procedure

1. The students should view the video and take notes. Put students in small groups.
2. The students will study the images produced in different regions of the state. Assign groups to the regions. A region may have more than one group working on it.
3. The students will create a catalog of the images. All references to dates will be notated. The students should also try to attach meanings to the images.
4. Each student will recreate an image to draw on the timeline. The images should be

drawn on the long sheet of craft paper to replicate the prehistoric art. Limit the size of the images.

5. After the drawings are completed, spray the chalk drawings with aerosol spray.
6. Then, write the meanings of the images that are represented on the timeline chart.
7. Discuss the timeline.

Evaluation

Did the students research the artwork? Did the students notice any differences and similarities in the styles of the images?

Art Reference Books

The art book (1998). London: Phaidon.

Janson, H. W. (1997). *The history of art.* New York: H. Abrams.

Strickland, C. & Boswell, J. (1992). *The annotated Mona Lisa: A crash course in art history from prehistoric to postmodern.* Kansas City: Andrews & McNeel.

Tansey, R. (1995). *Gardner's art through the ages.* New York: HBJ.

Probability & Statistics:
Fuel for Debate

I. Teacher Preparation

◆ **Background**
Time Required: 7–9 class periods

Getting Ready
For this lesson you will need the following:
- visuals (video clips, advertisements, print media) showing use of statistics in government and/or advertising.

Curriculum Standards

The student will:

Primary Standard
- Collect, organize, and display relevant data.

Embedded Content and Skills
- Use measure of central tendency and range to describe a set of data.
- Select and use an appropriate representation for presenting collected data and justify the selection.
- Describe a set of data using mean, median, mode, and range.
- Determine solution strategies and analyze or solve problems.
- Make inferences and convincing arguments based on an analysis of given or collected data.

Curriculum Standard Level:
Introductory X   Developmental   Extension

◆ Framework

Theme: Relationships

Generalization: Relationships may be used to dominate or maintain the status quo.

Content Focus: Probability and Statistics—students will learn how data is used for debate. (This includes the misuse of data.)

Rationale: The study of probability and statistics gives students insight into the persuasive use of numbers.

Differentiation Framework

Thinking Skills	Depth/Complexity	Research	Products
• Compare and contrast • Identify attributes • Recognize relationships • Summarize • State assumptions • Judge with criteria	• Details • Patterns • Rules • Different perspectives	• Internet resources • Media resources • Reference books • Interview	• Charts • Photo or picture essay • Dramatization

Thinking Skills

- **Compare and contrast**—note similarities and differences.
  Example: Students will compare statistics that are used.
- **Identify attributes**—describe qualities and characteristics.
  Example: Students will identify the persuasive use of data.
- **Recognize relationships**—understanding connections among different entities.
  Example: Students will relate the use of statistics for different purposes.
- **Judge with criteria**—evaluate based on standards.
  Example: Students will establish criteria and judge the validity of arguments.

Depth/Complexity

- **Details**—parts, attributes, factors, and variables.
  Example: Students will identify data that may be used as statistics for a variety of purposes.
- **Patterns**—repetition, predictability.
  Example: Students will note recurring patterns and trends in the use of data or information presented statistically.
- **Rules**—structure, order, hierarchy.
  Example: Students will use rules for debate in presenting material.

- **Different points of view**—multiple perspectives, opposing viewpoints, differing roles, and knowledge.
  Example: Students will demonstrate how the data can be used to prove differing opinions.

Research

Students will use a variety of reference resources, including the Internet, media resources, books, and interviews, to gather data for debate.

Product

Students will present results in the form of charts, photo essays, and/or dramatizations based on controversial issues from history and current events.

II. The Lesson

◆ Motivation

1. Show students video clips or print copies of advertisements, city council meeting, or news reports that involve the use of statistics as a method to persuade or influence opinions, interests, or actions. Discuss the covert and overt use of statistical data in each type of communication.

◆ Input

1. Ask students what ideas or examples can support the statement "Data may be used to facilitate, dominate, or maintain the status quo." Discuss key words to ensure understanding:
   - *data*—facts or figures;
   - *facilitate*—to assist or make easier;
   - *dominate*—to rule or control by superior power;
   - *maintain*—to keep the same; and
   - *status quo*—the existing state of affairs, how things are now.
2. Solicit meanings for the statement from the students.
3. Record the students' ideas about the meaning of the statement. *(Noting each student's name by his or her response will help facilitate scholarly discussion later. Students can then recall their peers' statements in a discussion.)*
4. Have students look for ideas and examples of how data is used and where to find information to support their ideas. On chart tablets or poster board, have groups record their information in two columns: Ideas/Examples and Where to Look.
5. Combine the information from small groups into one class chart.

◆ Output

- Select one of the ideas and examples from the class chart to research using multiple and varied references. Define the reasons data may be used as a facilitator, dominator, or neutralizer. Show that there are multiple functions for statistics using current newspaper articles reporting statistical data.

◆ Culmination

Students will participate in a debate using statistics to support their assigned point of view.

1. Divide the class into three groups of 10 students.

2. Separate the three large groups into pro and con groups of five students each.

3. Instruct the students about the ground rules for an intellectual debate (see Debate Guidelines on page 108).

4. Assign the debate teams an issue for debate (see Teacher Notes).

5. Allow time to conduct research and gather statistical data to present an argument or point of view.

6. Debate the issues in groups. Record results.

7. After the small-group debates, as a class discuss the use of statistics in debates using these questions:
   - Are the statistics necessary for a debate?
   - Do the statistics tell different stories if they are displayed in different forms?
   - Can statistics be misused?

8. Tie the newly gained knowledge back to the generalizations by asking the students to sustain, amend, or rebuff their ideas about the generalization: Relationships can be used to dominate or maintain the status quo.

Teacher Notes

1. Possible issues for debate:
   - Should the Census Bureau use statistical sampling in the census 2000?
   - Immigration—should the U.S. continue to allow large groups of people?
   - U.S. mail service and e-mail—will there be a need for the U.S. mail service in the future?
   - Violence in America—Is the entertainment industry to blame?
   - Is wilderness possible without stewardship?

2. Use Web sites for research, including *Newsweek, Time, USA Today, Science News, American Journal of Medicine, Consumer Report, Wall Street Journal*, major newspapers, and television network news sites.

3. Use your favorite search engine to locate debate Web sites. Check these Web sites to locate more ideas to debate.
   - http://www.historychannel.com
   - http://debate.uvm.edu/lobby.html
   - www.parl.gc.ca/36/1/parlbus/chambus/senate/deb-e/deb-e.htm
   - http://www.colorado.edu/cwa/

4. Here are a few books that may be good resources: *How to Lie With Statistics* by Danell Huff, *Designing Infographics* by Eric K. Meyer, *Tainted Truth: The Manipulation of Fact in America* by Cynthia Crosson.

◆ **Extensions**

—Independent Research Topics

Choose an historical debate from U.S. history in one of the following categories: environmental, medical, political, social, or scientific. Have students research the basis of the two sides and locate or reconstruct possible statistical evidence from the time period. In culmination, they will select the type of product that will best display the knowledge that they have acquired.

—Products

1. Survey and graph results of a study. Dramatize your findings as a statistician from the time period.
2. Make charts and develop a photo essay in the manner of a statistician's report similar to the time period.
3. Make a collection of various data charts and state an assumption about data collection.
4. Write and perform a talk radio show discussing your findings.
5. Write a journal of a person of the times to record the issues and statistics that were needed in their debate.
6. Write a news article about your findings.
7. Construct a presentation board. Present issues and statistics of various charts to represent pros and cons of the issue.

Debate Guidelines

- A debate consists of spoken arguments for and against a proposition, a statement that is carefully worded to make clear the positive and negative implications.

- A simplified debate includes the proposition, analysis (a careful study of the proposition), the case (developing positive or negative arguments), evidence (finding facts to support the arguments), and rebuttal (plan to attack the opposition's arguments).

- The traditional debate follows this format:

—Constructive Speeches

1. First affirmative argument
2. First negative argument
3. Second affirmative argument
4. Second negative argument

—Rebuttal speeches

1. First negative
2. First affirmative
3. Second negative
4. Second affirmative

The constructive speeches are usually twice as long as rebuttal speeches.

—Interdisciplinary Options

Students are to use statistics and write a news article to facilitate, dominate, or maintain a status quo about an issue listed below or any other issue that students may find relevant (see "Relationships: Using Statistics" Study Starter).

—Adaptations for Other Grade Levels

1. **Grade 6 and under:** Practice the rules of debating with an issue that is relevant to the times. For example: "Should the school have a soda machine in the cafeteria?" This will

allow the students to apply the rules of debate to an issue that is more concrete before applying it to the field of statistics.

2. **Grade 8–9:** Watch several debates. Analyze the components of the debate, noting details such as ethics and rules followed in the debate.

Relationships:
Using Statistics

Use statistics and write a news article to facilitate, dominate, or maintain a status quo about an issue listed below or any other issue that you may find relevant. The article must be in a news story format and use data to persuade the reader.

Issues

- Bilingual Abilities in Business Today

- Engineering Safe Buildings in Earthquake Areas of the World

- Believing Everything You Read: Media Coverage

- Cost vs. Culture: Should We Spend Money for a Community Symphony Hall (or play-house, or new library, or ballet company)?

- Community Growth: Major Industry: Is it Really Good for Our Economy?

- School Uniforms: Making School a Better Place or Infringing on Student Rights?

- Animal Experimentation for Medical Research

Compile the completed articles into a newspaper format using computer software. Make copies for all writers and for the library.

The Golden Mean

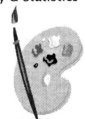

The use of proportion and ratio in probability and statistics is reflected in art's long interest in the perfect ratio.

The human body is a challenging subject to render artistically, especially if the goal is to render it realistically. An artist's main concern at the onset of such an endeavor is getting the correct proportions of the figure. That means that the size relationship of parts to each other looks correct. Proportion is important with regard to other forms of art, as well. An industrial designer must design furniture with the proper proportions to assure that the piece is going to function properly. Architects are also aware of the importance of proportion and how it determines the outcome of aesthetics and function.

A proportion can be expressed mathematically as a ratio. The Greek mathematician Euclid discovered what was thought to be the perfect ratio to represent the ideal proportion. This ratio is called the Golden Mean, or the Golden Section. The Greeks applied the Golden Mean to the making of both artwork and architecture. This application of a ratio formula has also been used in modern times. The Golden Section Rectangle is a visual representation of the Golden Mean. The ratio of the Golden Mean is 1 to 1.6. The sides of the rectangle correspond with the ratio. The facade of the Parthenon fits into the Golden Section Rectangle. The height of the columns related to the highest point of the facade also fits the 1:1.6 ratio. The measurement of the navel to the top of the head compared to the measurement of the navel to the feet is the ratio of 1:1.6.

Objective

The students will create Golden Section Rectangles using arbitrary dimensions. They will also create designs by applying the ratio.

Materials

- White drawing paper 12" x 18"
- pencils
- rulers
- erasers
- colored markers

Procedure

1. The students should select a dimension and multiply it by 1.6. If the dimension is 8 inches, the longest side of the rectangle will measure 12.8." The resulting rectangle will measure 8" x 12.8."
2. Draw the Golden Section Rectangle. Now create a square within the rectangle by drawing another 8-inch line 8 inches from one short side of the rectangle and parallel to the short sides of the rectangle. The resulting rectangle will be another Golden Section Rectangle.
3. Repeat this step once more within this new Golden Section Rectangle. Start by measuring the length of the short sides. Then create the square using the dimensions of the short sides. Once again, the result will be a square within the Golden Section Rectangle

and a new and smaller Golden Section Rectangle.

4. Continue the process until measuring becomes difficult. The students should use colored markers to add color and patterns to their design. Regardless of the various sizes the students began with, all the designs will look proportionately the same.

Evaluation

Did the students demonstrate understanding of the ratio relationship of the sides of the rectangle? Was the design well executed?

Art Reference Books

The art book (1998). London: Phaidon.

Janson, H. W. (1997). *The history of art.* New York: H. Abrams.

Strickland, C. & Boswell, J. (1992). *The annotated Mona Lisa: A crash course in art history from prehistoric to postmodern.* Kansas City: Andrews & McNeel.

Tansey, R. (1995). *Gardner's art through the ages.* New York: HBJ.

Ecological Succession

I. Teacher Preparation

◆ **Background**
Time Required: 5–10 class periods

Getting Ready
For this lesson you will need the following:
- *Bay Shore Park: The Death and Life of an Amusement Park* by Victoria Crenson;
- *From Pond to Prairie* by Laurence Pringle; and
- reproductions of M. C. Escher prints.

Curriculum Standards

The student will:

Primary Standard
- Understand the relationship between organisms and the environment.

Embedded Content and Skills
- Chart the relationship between structure and function in living systems.
- Interpret the responses of organisms caused by internal or external stimuli.
- Analyze the relationship between organisms and the environment.
- Explain how natural events and human activity can alter Earth systems.

Curriculum Standard Level:
Introductory X   Developmental   Extension

◆ Framework

Theme: Relationships

Generalization: Relationships change over time.

Content Focus: Students will write a narrative to describe the meaning of ecological succession.

Rationale: The study of ecological succession gives students insight into the life cycles of plants and animals and the gradual changes involved in primary and secondary succession.

Differentiation Framework

Thinking Skills	Depth/Complexity	Research	Products
• Sequence • Recognize relationships	• Language of discipline • Details • Patterns	• Reference books • Internet sources	• Ecological timeline

Thinking Skills

- **Sequence**—to relate to another; to form a pattern.
  Example: Students will sequence the changes in regional development of communities.
- **Recognize relationships**—to recognize the connections among different entities.
  Example: Students will identify relationships between plants and animals associated with specific environments.

Depth/Complexity

- **Language of the discipline**—specialized vocabulary; tools used by the discipline.
  Example: Students will incorporate the language of the discipline in their narratives.
- **Details**—the essential facts and data.
  Example: Students will utilize the details of the discipline in understanding concepts.
- **Patterns**—to define the repetition; predictability of a sequence.
  Example: Students will predict changes in organisms as a result of natural events.

Research

Read and use reference sources to collect data, organize information, and draw conclusions.

Product

Students will create an ecological timeline to depict the process of ecological succession.

II. The Lesson

◆ Motivation

1. Use one of the following titles as a text with a large or small group of students. Books could also be used as individualized reading material:
    * *Bay Shore Park: The Death and Life of an Amusement Park* by Victoria Crenson;
    * *How the Forest Grew* by William Jasperson; or
    * *Summer of Fire: Yellowstone 1988* by Patricia Lauber.
    Ask the students to summarize the main idea of the book.
2. Have the students identify relationships within the story. Post these on a class chart or small group charts.
3. Use the following questions as the basis of discussing the relationship of the book read by the students to the concepts of the lesson:
    * How did the author(s) portray the relationship between organisms and the environment?
    * How did the main idea(s) of the book support the concept that structure and function are related?
    * How did the book prove that an ecological succession occurs?
4. Conduct an experiment that illustrates the main ideas described in the reading materials. Ask students to locate evidence from their books that show and tell in words what was exemplified in the experiment. (Consider having students summarize the main idea(s) from the book they read in an "experiment book report.")
5. Present students with the following chart.

Theme: Relationships Generalization: Relationships change over time		
Proof from our readings		
Bay Shore	*Forest Grew*	*Summer Fire*

6. Discuss the differences between inductive and deductive reasoning. Instruct students that they will be proving deductively the meaning of the generalization by gathering details from their readings. (Note that details to prove, clarify, and define the generalization are derived from only the resources or books read by the students.) Examine the completed chart depicting the details to identify a pattern within, between, or across books.
7. Use the chart to initiate or discuss studies of ecological succession.

◆ Input

* Create an environmental community in an aquarium or terrarium. Add and/or subtract specific elements to the environment on a regularly scheduled plan. Define the changes in the relationship between the organisms and the environment over time. Describe the details and patterns of change in a journal or illustrate them for presentation in a timeline.

◆ Output

1. Distribute copies of *From Pond to Prairie* by Laurence Pringle to read in small groups. If multiple copies are not available, read the selection to the class. If this book is not available, use a similar title.

2. Distribute "Relationships: Ecological Succession" Study Starter to groups. Instruct the students to complete the chart about relationships in ecological succession.

3. Set up research stations based on the following topics of ecological succession:
   - Sand Dunes of Lake Michigan;
   - Glacier Bay National Park (Alaska);
   - Mt. St. Helens Since May 1980;
   - Yellowstone Forest Fire 1988;
   - Floods and Fires of California; and
   - Hurricane Andrew (or other storm) Devastation of the Forest in the Eastern U.S.
   Research stations can consist of print and other reference materials, pictures, and materials for student projects.

4. Use the same chart for all groups and provide a variety of materials for research at each station. Use these other major themes as prompts to explain the phenomenon at each research station:
   - Cycles (lunar, water, seasonal, photosynthesis);
   - Systems (digestive, circulatory, reproductive, respiratory); and
   - Symbiosis (mutualism).

◆ Culmination

1. Instruct students to make a documentary in the form of an ecological timeline that shows how relationships change over time with information relating to their research topic. Timelines should show primary and secondary succession. Presentations may be on an exhibit board with photographs, drawings, and/or video, or may be on a computer program.

Teacher Notes

Ecological succession—the slow, regular sequence of changes in the regional development of communities of plants and associated animals, culminating in a climax characteristic of a specific geographical environment.

Producer—any of various organisms (e.g., a green plant) that produce their own organic compounds from simple precursors (e.g., carbon dioxide and inorganic nitrogen) and many of which are food sources for other organisms.

Consumer—an organism requiring complex organic compounds for food, which it obtains by preying on other organisms or by eating particles of organic matter.

Decomposer—any of various organisms (e.g., many bacteria and fungi) that return constituents of organic substances to ecological cycles by feeding on and breaking down dead protoplasm.

Primary Succession—the processes involved in changing an area from one lacking any community of plants or animals to one consisting of individuals and ecosystems.

Secondary Succession—the arrival of a new species in an area that already has life.

2. Present these projects to the class and note similarities and differences. Summarize by proving the generalization: Relationships change over time.

◆ Extensions

—Independent Research Topics

1. Investigate the work of the philosopher Jean-Jacques Rousseau to find a relationship between beliefs about ecology and the actual ecological events occurring in our environment.

2. Research local examples of ecological succession, such as an abandoned rock quarry, gravel pit, logging sites, small town area, sand dunes, or new lakes developed for local water reservoirs. Create a documentary in the form an ecological timeline showing primary and secondary secessions. Set up your documentary for exhibit at a local natural history museum, community museum, court house, chamber of commerce, or library.

—Interdisciplinary Options

1. **Social Studies (Geography)**: Map volcanic activity in the world and describe the different types of ecological succession and changes that occur due to the various climates at these locations.

2. **Language Arts/Mathematics**: Research and form statistical data to persuade the city council not to let a large manufacturing company or amusement park industry build on a wilderness site in your county.

3. **Speech/Mathematics**: Debate whether modern technologies should be used to stop forest fires in wilderness areas or whether they should be allowed to burn themselves out. Show charts and data to support your view.

—Classical Connections

- **Current Events**: Investigate global warming as it applies to ecological succession. Describe the changes in the plant and animal life of a selected biome that could occur from a rise in temperature.

Relationships:
Ecological Succession

Define the Relationships	Describe the Details	Identify the Patterns	Explain the types of Changes

Metamorphosis:
Inanimate to Animate

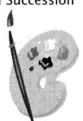

*Art transformations can provide a visual representation
of evolutionary change in the environment.*

M. C. Escher's prints are very popular today. That was not the case during the early days of his career. He was born in Holland in 1898. After completing high school, he entered architectural school and transferred to the graphic art department. His artistic quest was to visualize many worlds existing at the same time. He spent much of his time pursuing his quest with little financial reward. In 1968, M. C. Escher's prints received critical attention in a Holland museum. From that point on, his prints were famous worldwide. Escher died in 1972. Today, his prints can be seen on T-shirts, greeting cards, posters, and many other items. His unique style of art created other worlds of transformations and ambiguous dimensions.

Objective

The students will create a drawing of an inanimate object that evolves into an animate object. The students will include a shading technique in the drawing.

Materials

- white drawing paper 12" x 18"
- pencils
- erasers
- practice drawing paper 12" x 18"
- inanimate objects (clothes pins, small toys, combs, and other objects that can be placed on a desk to draw)
- *Design Synectics* by Nicholas Roukes

Procedure

1. The students will divide the 12" x 18" practice paper into four equal parts by folding the paper in half, making two 12" x 9" sections. Then fold the folded paper in half once more into 12" x 4½" sections. Unfold the paper, and you should have four 12" x 4½" sections.
2. Working from left to right, draw the inanimate object in the left section. The finished animate object should be drawn in the section at the right end of the paper. The spaces in between should show the gradual transformation of the inanimate object into the animate object. Try transforming a tire into a snail or a computer mouse into a rat. Be sure to use the practice paper before attempting the finished drawing.
3. Finally, the students should add shading to their drawings so that the finished objects appear to be three-dimensional.

Art Reference Books

The art book. (1998). London: Phaidon.

Janson, H. W. (1997). *The history of art.* New York: H. Abrams.

Strickland, C. & Boswell, J. (1992). *The annotated Mona Lisa: A crash course in art history from prehistoric to postmodern.* Kansas City: Andrews & McNeel.

Tansey, R. (1995). *Gardner's art through the ages.* New York: HBJ.

Eighth GRADE

Theme: Power

- Language Arts—Scarlett, Scalawags, and Southern Society
- Social Studies—Threads of Revolution
- Math—Probability & Statistics: Making Decisions
- Science—Extinction

Scarlett, Scalawags, & Southern Society

I. Teacher Preparation

◆ Background
Time Required: 6–9 weeks

Getting Ready
For this lesson you will need the following:
- Margaret Mitchell's *Gone With the Wind*;
- reproduction of Picasso's *Guernica*; and
- newspapers and art supplies.

Curriculum Standards

The student will:

Primary Standard
- Recognize how features of a genre build understanding of the human experience.

Embedded Content and Skills
- Draw inferences or generalizations and support with textual evidence.
- Interpret text ideas through journal writing and discussion.
- Analyze characters, including their traits, motivations, conflicts, points of view, relationships, and changes they undergo.
- Produce cohesive and coherent written texts by organizing ideas, using effective transitions, and choosing precise wording.

Curriculum Standard Level:
Introductory   Developmental   **Extension X**

◆ Framework

Theme: Power

Generalization: Different forms and uses of power result in conflict. There are many types of power—individual, political, monetary, physical, and so forth. The manner in which individuals and groups use power often causes conflict, and this conflict sometimes leads to changes.

Content Focus: Historical fiction—students determine the relevance of historical fiction to understanding lifestyles and attitudes before, during, and after the Civil War.

Rationale: The study of historical fiction gives students insight into the lifestyles and attitudes of a particular time and allows them to see that people encounter similar problems across cultures and throughout time. One of these problems relates to the use of power—personal, physical, financial, spiritual, and political. It is important for gifted students to understand how power can be used wisely as a change agent and how the abuse of power can result in conflict and loss, as this will play a role in their own lives.

Differentiation Framework

Thinking Skills	Depth/Complexity	Research	Products
• Hypothesize • Identify characteristics/attributes • Determine cause/effect	• Language of discipline • Point of view • Ethics • Establish interdisciplinary connections • Changes over time	• Draw conclusions about Civil Wars in other countries • Internet sources	• Analytical journal • Art product

Thinking Skills

- **Hypothesize**—to form an explanation.
  Example: Students will compare art products and will hypothesize the theme based on the existing information/clues. Students will hypothesize character motivation.
- **Identify characteristics/attributes**—note features, qualities.
  Example: Students will identify the characteristics of historical fiction. Students will identify personality attributes of characters in the book.
- **Determine cause/effect**—examine reasons for occurrences.
  Example: Students will determine the causes of characters' actions within the story and the results of those actions.

Depth/Complexity

- **Language of the discipline**—specialized vocabulary, tools used by the discipline.
  Example: Students will identify and apply the language and tools of a sociologist or psychologist in their journals.

- **Patterns**—repetition; predictability.
  Example: Students will hypothesize characters' reactions to conflict and the theme of personal and group power based on their previous behaviors.
- **Ethics**—different opinions; judging.
  Example: Students will determine the causes and effects of the use of power by individuals and groups.
- **Establish interdisciplinary connections**—relationships between and across disciplines.
  Example: Students will identify the characteristics and attributes of politics and human behavior as a reflection of personal/societal attitudes. Students will determine the causes and effects of interrelationships between history and literature, especially from the perspective of the disciplines of a sociologist and psychologist.
- **Over time-relationships**—between past, present, and future; relationships within a time period.
  Example: Students will identify characteristics and attributes of humankind's use of power during the time surrounding the Civil War and relate how this use of power has impacted relationships and politics within the U.S. as a result.

Research

Students will research to draw conclusions about common causes of civil wars across societies. Students will research to discover the language of the discipline and tools of sociologists and psychologists.

Product

Students will create an art project that reflects their view of the theme of power. Students will write an analytical journal discussing the use of individual and group power in *Gone With the Wind* using the language of a sociologist or psychologist.

II. The Lesson

◆ Motivation

1. Discuss why and how people use power within a school, home, a society, and among societies. Ask students how power can be used in a positive or negative fashion. Have students research power in a dictionary and in a thesaurus to develop broad definition of power and to validate their responses.
2. Instruct each student to create an art project that reflects his or her view of the theme of power (see "The Power of Art" Study Starter for directions).
3. Presentation/hypothesizing
   - Have each student share his or her art project with the class. Inform students that they are to hypothesize about the theme—power—in the art projects shared.
   - Categorize the types of power students identified in the art projects shared by their peers: physical, psychological, political, military, and so forth.
   - Use the list or chart of the various types of power to evoke a discussion about their attitudes regarding these forms of power.

- Ask students to discuss the factors contributing to their attitudes.
4. Discuss historical fiction with students:
  - Ask students to define historical fiction. Ask them to recall the features of the genre from their previous studies. Use the concept of comparative analysis to clarify the elements or features of historical fiction by comparing it to a previously learned genre.
  - Introduce students to costume romance since this is probably not a term they have heard previously (see Teacher Notes).
  - Ask students to give examples of historical fiction and costume romances that they have read. Ask them which they liked better and why.
  - Inform students they will be reading the historical fiction novel *Gone With the Wind* to explore the concept of power.

◆ Input
1. Parallel the study of the Civil War to the reading of *Gone With the Wind* by collegial or team planning between history and language arts teachers.

Teacher Notes

Definition of historical fiction
- A novel or short story that has a setting during a particular time or over a long period of time in history (usually one of great conflict).
- It relates the social and/or political conditions of the period.
- It reflects the attitudes, clothing and home styles, manners, and other details of life of the time period.
- It may have characters who actually lived at that time.
- It shows how people were impacted by the events of that time.
- It often demonstrates changes in the society as a result of the conflict.

Costume romance is historical fiction that has very little factual historic basis. These stories merely use the setting of a particular time or place to tell the story of an individual with very little historical accuracy.

Civil War (1861–1865)—It is important that students realize that slavery was one of many causes of the war. The war was fought over tremendous differences in the social and economic structure of the North and South. Slavery was one aspect of the social reform movements of the time. Most Northerners fought primarily to keep the country united and because of their sense of national loyalty.

Reconstruction (1865–1877)—This is the time period in which the Confederacy was brought back into the U.S. Many conflicts arose during Reconstruction, especially after the assassination of Lincoln. There was a great deal of disagreement as to what rights and powers the Southerners would maintain or lose. Some Northerners felt that the South should be punished for starting the war, while others were more empathetic and less adversarial. Lincoln wanted the South brought back into the nation quickly and with charity. As a result of the harsh

2. Ask students to define civil war (a war between political factions or regions within a country) and revolution (an overthrow of a government or social system). Discuss the concepts of civil wars around the world and throughout different time periods: Kosovo, '60s in the U.S., and so forth. Extend the discussion to compare civil wars with revolutions.

3. Discuss the disciplines of psychology and sociology. based on their previous knowledge. Infer the roles of a psychologist and sociologist.

Teacher Notes—Con't

Republican approach to Reconstruction after Lincoln's death, the Republicans lost favor among the former Southern landowners, but were popular among the newly freed slaves. The Ku Klux Klan and other racist groups formed as a result of the former landowners' hostile feelings.

Locate a copy of "50 Years of *Gone with the Wind*" by Roy Meador, published in the September 1986 issue of *Civil War Times Illustrated*. It provides excellent background information about Margaret Mitchell and the historic background to the book. The students should read the book before reading this article.

- Provide students time to research the roles of psychologist and sociologist, using both the Internet and print references.
- Give them blank "Think Like a Psychologist" and "Think Like a Sociologist" Study Starters and have them fill in the blanks. See the Teacher Notes versions (teacher answer copy) to help guide students. (Students may research individually, in pairs and share results with their partner, or in groups and present their findings to the class.) Direct students to research to discover:
  - what the disciplines of sociology and psychology are;
  - what skills psychologists and sociologists use;
  - what terminology is specific to that job; and
  - what types of products people in these professions use to do their work.
- Discuss the responses they included on the students chart to validate that the student information is relevant and accurate.

◆ Output

1. Tell students they will read *Gone with the Wind* and define and exemplify the use of power in the book from the perspective of a psychologist or a sociologist.
   - Distribute the "Think Like a Psychologist/Sociologist *Gone With the Wind* Journal Assignment" Study Starter.
   - Discuss the positive and negative consequences of viewing things (paintings, current events, novels, etc.) from different perspectives. Discuss differences and similarities of viewing things from the different perspectives internal to the novel, such as characters, or external to the novel, such as critics, publishers, and so forth. Have students identify a perspective and use it to write a three-part journal entry from the perspective of a psychologist or sociologist.

- If they choose to be a psychologist, they will be analyzing Scarlett O'Hara's behavior and how the concept of power plays a role in her development, as well as her relationships with other characters throughout the book.
- If they choose to look at the book as a sociologist, they will be studying which groups have power, how they use power, and how the various groups react to shifts in power throughout the book.

Journal Evaluation/Assessment

Students will be graded on:
- thoroughness and depth of thought reflected in the analysis;
- supporting ideas with examples from the book;
- proper use of the language of the discipline used in the analysis;
- ability to work independently; and
- proper sentence structure, grammar, and spelling.

- Tell the students to use the "Think like a Psychologist" or "Think Like a Sociologist" Study Starter, which they filled in to guide them as they read and write.

2. Read "50 Years of *Gone With the Wind*" by Roy Meador, published in the September 1986 issue of *Civil War Times Illustrated,* after completing the novel.

3. Discuss these topics or areas:
   - **Small-group discussion**—Have students generate questions relating to the social and personal rules and patterns of behavior, how varying points of view and biases are reflected in the book, and how the concept of power caused rules to be broken and create new patterns of behavior. Pair or group students so that there is a mix of psychologists and sociologists. Have them discuss their questions in a small group. Remind them that there are no wrong answers as long as they can support them with explicit evidence from the book.
   - **Seminar format**—See "Student Seminar" Study Starter in the "Mysteries, We Write" unit for seventh-grade language arts and hold a class seminar using the dual circle technique of discussion. Students will generate the questions and lead the discussion.
   - **Teacher-led discussion**. Possible questions include:
     - What patterns of behavior were evident in Scarlett early in the book?
     - Which patterns and trends in her personality/behavior changed as the story progressed? Explain. Why did these change and others remain constant? What caused those patterns to change?
     - Which details of Scarlett's character traits are admirable?
     - Once Scarlett made her final "discovery," how do you think her behavior would change if the book continued?
     - How did Scarlett's attitudes and behavior patterns differ from other political/social groups? How did the attitudes and perspectives of various groups (former landowners, slaves, women on the home front, soldiers) change (or did they?) as the war progressed?
     - What biases over time caused those patterns in behavior?
     - How did the end of the war impact those attitudes and behavior or create ethical issues?

- Who (individuals and groups) had power and what types of power were evident in the book? From which perspectives was the power used wisely?
- How did individuals and groups react to this use of power?
- How did the political and social structure change as the power shifted? What factors allowed that to take place?

◆ Culmination
—Class discussion

1. Why is this book considered a classic? What evidence can you use to support your belief?
2. How does the point of view of this book affect the way history is represented?
3. What value does it have historically?
4. What did you learn about the Civil War and human behavior from reading this book?
5. What is the difference between a civil war and a revolution? If the South had won the Civil War, what would this war have been called?
6. Did the Civil War or the period of Reconstruction have more impact on racial tension in the South in the 20th century? Explain.
7. Have these perspectives and behaviors changed in recent decades? Explain.
8. How has this impacted the U.S.'s political structure?
9. In U.S. society today, who holds the power? Why? What causes the balance of power to change?
10. How do the rules of power within a country or society or social circle change over time?
11. When does one person's power or one group's power become abusive? What rules limit power? What types of rules should exist in relationship to power?
12. Have you or someone you know ever abused power? What happened as a result? (This would make a good writing assignment.)
13. What kinds of power do you as individuals have? How do you or the people around you use power?

NOTE: It might be interesting to discuss with students how these same themes of power and its uses dominate the science fiction genre.

◆ Extensions
—Independent Research Topics
—Interdisciplinary Options
Individual Research That Leads to Class Discussion

Assign each student to research a country that has experienced civil war. Every student should have a different country or at least a different civil war. (Some countries have experienced several civil wars.) Try to have countries from all parts of the world. Have them research only to discover the causes of the war and the outcome of the war, not the war itself.

1. Have students share the causes of war on the board, an overhead transparency, or chart.
   - Analyze the data to determine the most common causes of civil war.
   - Prioritize the list from most to least significant.
2. Have students share the outcomes of the civil wars on the board, an overhead transparency, or chart.

- Make generalizations about the results of the civil war. For example: 1) a change in type of government and rules within a country; and 2) a continuing series of civil wars over the struggle for power.
- Discuss what factors could prevent civil wars.

—Independent Research Projects

Each student will research and create a product or presentation that demonstrates his or her findings.

1. Research a country (other than the U.S.) or countries that have experienced civil war and analyze the causes and results of that war. What points of view existed and how was power used and/or abused?
2. Research the history of the Ku Klux Klan (or any other similar group that was formed to resist the use of power) and how its function and power have changed over time.
3. Research the history of the Democratic and Republican parties and the impact the Civil War and Reconstruction had on their political power and influence.
4. Debate whether countries like the U.S. or organizations like NATO should use their power and influence and become involved in disputes within a foreign country.
5. Research medical practices during the American Civil War.
6. Research Matthew Brady and photography of the Civil War and create a display of photographs.

—Classical Connections

Have students read an historical fiction short story or novel about a country other than the United States that experienced civil war (e.g., Hemingway's *For Whom the Bell Tolls*, Pasternak's *Doctor Zhivago*, or *Zlata's Diary*). Have them describe how the use of power is reflected in the piece of literature. How did power lead to war and/or resolve the conflict? What rules within the society changed as a result of the change in power or how did the use of power change? What new patterns and trends evolved? How did this impact the individuals involved?

NOTE: Several of these novels have movie versions, and, if time doesn't allow for the reading of the novel, show the movie and discuss the concepts above.

Philosophy

John Locke stated that "All men are equal … they have rights that cannot be taken away by society." How would Scarlett have responded to this? Mammy? Rhett Butler?

—Adaptations for Other Grade Levels

1. **Elementary**—Choose an historical fiction book such as Carolyn Meyer's *White Lilacs* that is more appropriate for their reading level. Go over the features of the genre and have students discuss how power was used and how the incidents reflected in the story caused changes within the country/society.
2. **High School**—Students read two historical fiction books (or even an historical fiction and a nonfiction book) relating to a given time period in a country, but told from different perspectives. For example: *Gone With the Wind* and *My Bondage and My Freedom* by Frederick Douglas, Harriet Beecher Stowe's *Uncle Tom's Cabin*, or *Cold Mountain* by

Charles Frazier. (Read the novels first to be sure parents in your school wouldn't object to the content.) Have students look at how the point of view affects the way each story is told. Have students focus on the theme of power and how the use of power is perceived; they can focus on the theme of conflict and how conflict causes changes in power structure and, therefore, changes in rules.

The Power of Art

Artists express ideas without using words. For this assignment, you will be an artist and express your idea(s) about **POWER** without using words.

- You must create some type of art project that represents your view of the theme of power.

- You may use any medium. You may sculpt, paint, create a collage or mobile, and so forth.

- On a note card or sheet of paper, write the main idea of your artwork.

If you have trouble coming up with a main idea related to the theme of power, talk to your parents about the definition of power or look up power in a book of quotations and locate a quote that reflects your personal attitudes.

Evaluation/Assessment

Grading will be based on these factors:

- ❏ How well the art reflects the written theme

- ❏ Artistic effort

- ❏ Ability to think and work independently

- ❏ Following directions

- ❏ Neatness

Think Like a Psychologist/Sociologist
Journal Assignment

Read *Gone With the Wind* and define and describe it from the perspective of a psychologist or a sociologist. You will write a three-part journal from the perspective of a psychologist or sociologist.

Psychologist

1. If you choose to be a psychologist, you will be defining Scarlett O'Hara's behavior. Describe how the concept of power plays a role in her development throughout the various time periods of the book. That is, what powers does she have? How does she use those powers? Why and how do her powers change or evolve? When and how does she use and/or abuse her power? How do other people react to her use of power? Is she justified in her actions?
2. The three parts of the journal will cover the following time periods or sections of the book:
    *   prewar (antebellum) and Scarlett's first marriage and widowhood;
    *   as the war continues—Scarlett's escape from Atlanta and her return to Tara and her marriage to her second husband; and
    *   from the death of her second husband and through her marriage to Rhett Butler.

Sociologist

1. If you choose to look at the book as a sociologist, you will be studying which groups have power and how they use power to affect the dynamics of interactions in the group. Also describe how the various groups (landowners, slaves, lower class, women, Northerners, military, etc.) react to shifts in power throughout the book.
2. The three parts of the journal will cover the following time periods or sections of the book:
    *   prewar (antebellum) and very early war years;
    *   as the war escalates and to its completion; and
    *   reconstruction.

Use your "Think Like a Psychologist" or "Think Like a Sociologist" Study Starter to guide you as you read and write.

1. You may create tests, write observation journals, conduct interviews, analyze statistics, or create questionnaires, graphs, or charts that a sociologist or psychologist would use in compiling information to prepare the analysis. Be sure to use the terminology or language of the discipline.

2. Your journal must have a cover page that includes your name, your "job title," date, and your purpose in writing the journal. (Stay in character. Think about why the psychologist or sociologist would be creating this document.)

Evaluation/Assessment: You will be graded on:

- thoroughness and depth of thought reflected in your analysis;
- supporting your ideas with examples from the book;
- proper use of the language of the discipline used in your analysis;
- ability to work independently; and
- proper sentence structure, grammar, and spelling.

Due Date: _____

Gone With the Wind:
A Study of Power
Think Like a Psychologist

Directions: Complete this form as a means of getting acquainted with the professional roles and responsibilities of a psychologist.

1. Think like a psychologist, or one who studies _____

   _____

2. Identify the language of a psychologist to describe what you are studying: _____

   _____

   _____

3. List the products created by a psychologist: _____

   _____

   _____

4. Define the skills of a psychologist: _____

   _____

   _____

Gone With the Wind:
A Study of Power
Think Like a Sociologist

Directions: Complete this form as a means of getting acquainted with the professional roles and responsibilities of a sociologist.

1. Think like a sociologist, or one who studies_____

    _____

2. Identify the language of a sociologist to describe what you are studying: _____

    _____

    _____

3. List the products created by a sociologist: _____

    _____

    _____

4. Define the skills of a sociologist: _____

    _____

    _____

Think Like a Psychologist—Possible Answers

1. Think like a psychologist, or one who studies mental processes and behavior including motivation, thinking, learning, and feeling.
2. Identify the language of a psychologist to describe what you are studying:
   - behavior
   - thought processes
   - cognition
   - relationships
   - feelings
3. List the products created by a psychologist:
   - tests
   - questionnaires
   - observation
   - journals
   - statistics
   - interviews
4. Define skills of a psychologist::
   - observe
   - interpret
   - gather data
   - reason
   - formulate theories or principles

Think Like a Sociologist—Possible Answers

1. Think like a sociologist, or one who studies groups and how people behave as members of groups. Sociologists study groups, families, cultures, workers, and so forth.
2. Identify the language of a sociologist to describe what you are studying:
   - group dynamics
   - leadership
   - demographics
   - socialization
3. List the products created by a sociologist::
   - graphs
   - charts
   - debates (pros/cons)
   - journals
4. Define the skills of a sociologist:
   - observe
   - summarize
   - describe
   - relate
   - interpret

Pablo Picasso's
Guernica

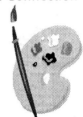

Visual art can be a powerful means
of communicating emotional events in history and contemporary society.

On Monday, April 26, 1937, the town of Guernica, a small Basque town in northern Spain, was bombed by the Nazi Luftwaffe in support of General Franco's fascist efforts during the Spanish Civil War. Prior to this horrific event, Pablo Picasso was commissioned to create a large mural for the Spanish Pavilion at the International Exposition. On May 1, 1937, Picasso saw three published photographs of the devastating episode of the Civil War. The casualties were 1,654 dead and 889 wounded. The victims consisted of mostly women, children, and older people.

These powerful images moved him to begin work on the 11½ x 24½ foot mural. He began drawing numerous abstract images of the devastation, suffering, cruelty, and menacing presence of war. Picasso created grotesquely distorted images, which he painted using a limited palette of black, white, and gray. The colors gave the mural a newspaper-like appearance, which was, after all, the medium that brought the news to Picasso. *Guernica* is a metaphor for humanity's brutality—a masterpiece of social art.

Objective
The students will create a collage that illustrates a reading of fiction or nonfiction.

Materials
- Newspapers
- Magazines
- Photographs
- Drawings
- Colored markers
- Crayons
- White glue
- Scissors
- Pencils
- Poster board

Procedure
1. Determine the size of the composition. One sheet of poster board can be cut into 2 or 4 pieces.
2. The students will decide upon a topic related to an emotional event in history or fiction. Students will illustrate this topic using the collage technique. The students will use this technique because it lends itself to a fragmented and distorted imagery.
3. The students will cut out images that will communicate their thoughts relating to their selected topics. They should include both print and pictures. Refer to the distorted and abstract imagery in Picasso's *Guernica*.

4. Limit the colors to black, white, and gray. Printed sections from newspaper and magazines can be used to represent shapes within the compositions. Picasso created the illusion of printed newspaper by painting patterns on the canvas.

5. After the composition is glued, complete the composition by adding markings using markers, crayons, or pencils.

Evaluation

Did the students effectively create a composition that illustrates the selected topic? Did the student successfully use the collage technique? Did the student distort an abstract printed imagery to communicate the thought?

Art Reference Books

The art book (1998). London: Phaidon.

Janson, H. W. (1997). *The history of art.* New York: H. Abrams.

Strickland, C. & Boswell, J. (1992). *The annotated Mona Lisa: A crash course in art history from prehistoric to postmodern.* Kansas City: Andrews & McNeel.

Tansey, R. (1995). *Gardner's art through the ages.* New York: HBJ.

Threads of Revolution

I. Teacher Preparation

◆ **Background**
Time Required: 3 weeks

Getting Ready
For this lesson you will need the following:
- *The Butter Battle Book* by Dr. Seuss;
- copies of the Declaration of Independence;
- copies of the Declaration of the Rights of Man and the Citizen; and
- supplies for creating picture books.

Curriculum Standards

The student will:

Primary Standard
- Analyze causes of the American Revolution, including the questions of power, authority, governance, and economic issues.

Embedded Content and Skills
- Understand traditional historical points of reference in U.S. history.
- List the foundations of representative government in the United States.
- Explain the locations and characteristics of places and regions of the United States, past and present.
- Understand the origins and development of the free enterprise system in the United States.
- Explain important American beliefs reflected in the U.S. Constitution and other documents.
- Understand the importance of the Founding Fathers as models of civic virtue.

Curriculum Standard Level:
Introductory X   Developmental   Extension

◆ Framework

Theme: Power

Generalization: Power, or the abuse of power, is a tool for revolution.

Content Focus: Both the American and French Revolutions used power to create change.

Rationale: Through the analysis and discussions of both the American and French Revolutions, students use the concept of revolution as structure for the identification and examination of power struggles, such as westward expansion and the temperance movement, throughout American history.

Differentiation Framework

Thinking Skills	Depth/Complexity	Research	Products
• Discriminate similar/different • Determine cause/effect • Note ambiguity	• Trends • Ethics • Relationships over time	• Primary source documents, reference materials	• Original humorous children's book

Thinking Skills

*   **Discriminate similar/different**—to analyze things in terms of their likenesses (same) or their differences (not the same).
    Example: Students will create a Venn diagram that compares/contrasts the Declaration of Independence to the Declaration of the Rights of Man and the Citizen.
*   **Determine cause/effect**—to define the relationship between why things occur and the consequence of their occurrences.
    Example: Students will relate reasons why revolution brings about feelings of nationalism.
*   **Note ambiguity**—to investigate gaps, missing elements, and discrepancies in texts, pictures, and speeches.
    Example: Students will take a stand on the topic: The French Revolution was a failure while the American Revolution was a great success.

Depth/Complexity

*   **Trends**—the influences, forces, direction, or course of action present in a particular context.
    Example: Students will identify common factors and influences that may be present to cause a revolution.
*   **Ethics**—what is considered to be right or wrong in a situation or event.
    Example: Students will analyze both positive and negative uses of power to create change.

- **Relationships over time**—the relationship of events between past, present, and future or within a time period.
  Example: Students will identify one type of power and analyze its effect on a past, present, and potential future conflict. Students will evaluate the effect of the American Revolution on the French Revolution.

Research

- **Conduct historical research**—to conduct a retrospective analysis of an area of study using multiple and varied archival data.
  Example: Students will investigate a topic by researching categories found on a conflict chart. Students will decide whether or not a conflict was justified.

Product

- **Create an original children's book**—to assume the role of a children's author communicating a serious theme and generalization in a manner that is humorous in nature.
  Example: Students will communicate information to verify a generalization about the use of power leading to conflict by writing a humorous children's book. The humorous book will use its characters, settings, and events to represent abstract concepts.

II. The Lesson

◆ Motivation

1. Share the following with students: Authors often write humorous literature to convey serious messages. The creative use of language, coupled with bold and humorous artwork, makes the plot of the book we are about to share easy to follow and enjoy.

2. Read aloud *The Butter Battle Book* to the class. Be sure to share the artwork with students.

3. Ask students to identify what they believe to be the themes of the book. (Theme is the overarching message or idea the author wishes to convey through a literary selection. It is not to be confused with plot—the sequence of events that tell the story.) As a class, have students complete the chart below.

Teacher Notes

The literature of Dr. Seuss provides an excellent springboard for discussion on many levels. *The Butter Battle Book* is an allegory for the arms race, distrust of different cultures, the importance of technology in war, destruction using "the bomb," and the role of patriotism and national pride.

The Butter Battle Book Theme Analysis	
Theme	Supporting Evidence

4. Define *power* (the ability to exercise control or influence others). Ask students to identify the role power played in this story. (Responses may include the power of technology for more destructive weapons, "The Powers That Be" who continually made the decisions to promote Grandpa and continue the fight, the power of prejudice to incite conflict, or other responses.) Relate the definition of power to the book.

◆ Input

1. Tell students that they will be identifying and determining the causes and effects of both the American and French revolutions. Instruct students that they will be investigating trends precipitating these revolutions. Place students in groups of four. Within each group, two students will be responsible for gathering information about the American Revolution, while the other two students will gather information about the French Revolution.

    • Ask students to hypothesize the concept of "revolution." Look up the term in various dictionaries. Make sure they understand revolution as a sudden, radical, or complete change.

- Distribute the "Conflict Chart" Study Starter to students. Review the categories of the chart. Discuss the relationship between power and conflict. Introduce the variables that cause conflict: economic, social, and political. Apply the concept of "conflict as an effect of power" to a previously learned historic event. Apply the concept of "economic, social, political conflict as an effect of power" to the *same* historic event. Discuss the relationship of prominent figures and major incidents as causes of economic, social, and political conflict. Apply these causes to a previously learned historical event. Complete a section of the "Conflict Chart" Study Starter with the class. Instruct students to use reference materials, including their textbooks, in order to complete the charts.

- Direct students to explain the information they have gathered for the "Conflict Chart" Study Starter to their remaining group members. Members of each group must be prepared to participate in a class discussion about each revolution.

- Conduct a class discussion by having all groups share the information they have gathered for their respective group charts. Indicate the ambiguities or inaccuracies in information or inconsistencies with the interpretation of events.

- Have each group revisit their research on the causes of the conflict. Their new task is to identify one prominent individual from each conflict who used power for positive results and one prominent individual from each conflict who abused his or her power. Provide materials for students to draw a portrait of each prominent individual and write a brief summary of how each used or abused power. These individuals will be placed on a famous/infamous list of revolutionary personalities.

Teacher Notes

This would make a great bulletin board. Students can plan and design the bulletin board and then post their famous/infamous revolutionary personalities on it. Personalities may include Colonel Banaste Tarleton (a.k.a. "The Butcher"), Peter Salem, Benedict Arnold, Charles Lee, Henry Hamilton, Marquis le Lafayette (fought in both revolutions), King George III, Light Horse Harry Lee, King Louis XVI, Jean-Paul Marat, Georges-Jacques Danton, Maximillien Robespierre, Francoise Voltaire, Denis Diderot, and Jean-Jacques Rousseau.

2. Distribute copies of the Declaration of Independence and the Declaration of the Rights of Man and the Citizen to students. Discuss the origin and purpose of each document. Read and discuss each document on its own. Next, have students compare and contrast the two documents by completing a Venn diagram.

Declaration of Independence / Declaration of the Rights of Man and the Citizen

- Ask the following questions in order to generate a class discussion. Use this discussion as a time to introduce the concept and techniques of the "art of discussion" and/or Socratic seminar.
    - What are some of the common ideas and beliefs that are found in both documents?
    - What ambiguities are noted within and between the documents?
    - What ethical issues are prevalent in each document?
    - How do these documents reflect the trends of the times?
    - To whom do these documents give power? Why?

3. Ask students to gather evidence to support the statement that the French Revolution is generally labeled a failure, while the American Revolution is labeled a success.
    - Have students defend or disagree with the following statement by writing an editorial for the newspaper *Revolution Weekly*. "The French Revolution was a failure, while the American Revolution was a great success."

Teacher Notes

Language Arts Connection: Have students work in pairs to write a point/counterpoint type of editorial commentary. Have one student agree with the statement and have the second student respond by taking an opposite point of view.

4. Introduce the concept of trends to students by reading and reviewing contemporary newspapers. Define trends (political, social, etc.) that precipitated the French Revolution. Use the following statement as the motivator for the discussion.
    "It was the French Revolution that impacted politics, thought, and culture around the world. Three powerful revolutionary ideas sprang from the French Revolution: liberalism (favors freedom of the individual, civil rights, and constitutional government); socialism (places property in the hands of government with the intent to make everyone work and distribute wealth equally); and nationalism (all people want to take part in the nation's affairs, a feeling of national identity and patriotism)."
    - Have students use the context clues to define the words.
    - Have students share their editorials with the class. As the editorials are shared, have students place information they have included in their editorials in the appropriate column of the following chart.

Revolutionary Ideas

Liberalism	Socialism	Nationalism
Example: The bourgeoisie opposed the power of the church and wanted more fairness for everyone.	*Example:* Labeling everyone citizens and wanting a government where all had jobs and everyone's basic needs were met.	*Example:* Creation of a tri-colored flag and national anthem.

5. Review the definition of revolution with students (a sudden, radical, or complete change). Lead students to understand that a revolution is not always a war or physical conflict. Have students brainstorm a list of types of revolutions. Record their thoughts on the chalkboard. Responses may include social revolutions such as the temperance movement, political revolutions such as the suffrage movement, revolutions in technology such as the Industrial Revolution, cultural revolutions such as trends in fashion, or economic revolutions such as the use of the Eurodollar. Have students identify trends that are common to most revolutions.

- Next, have students brainstorm a list of types of power that are positive or negative influences on revolutions. Responses may include the power of the pen, the power of education, the power of honesty, the power of propaganda, abuse of power by politicians, the power of love, the power of perseverance, the power of money, and so forth. Give examples of these uses and abuses of power and have students exemplify them as either positive or negative influences.

- Assign each student or group of students one type of power. Students will create a poster showing the effects of the selected power on a past, present, and potential future conflict. Include as criteria for the posters an example of ways in which that power was used as a tool for revolution and subsequent conflict.

◆ Output

- Have students assemble four-person groups. Give the following instructions.
  — First, identify the parts found in all books. Your book must follow the format of all published books. Also, a children's book must be especially concise and easy to understand. Carefully plan the age of the intended audience.
  — You will be creating a children's book with your groups that is humorous in nature. The characters, settings, and events will represent abstract concepts of some type of revolutionary idea or movement. The concept of power as a tool for revolution must be an integral part of the book.
  — First, your group must brainstorm ideas for the plot and the overarching theme of the book, then create a story map of the plot, and then develop the story.
  — Assign duties to each group member to guarantee that the assignment is done well and completed on time. Duties will include designing and creating the front and back covers, creating the artwork, coloring the artwork, typing the story, and creating specialty pages such as the copyright page or the dedication page.
  — Decide how the book will be bound.
  — Finally, bind the book.

◆ Culmination

- Have each group read the completed book to the class. Discuss each book with the class as it is read. Ask students to identify how power is used as a tool

Teacher Notes

Remind students that it is important that they spend time correctly using the writing process. Stories should be well developed with no significant errors in grammar or mechanics.

along with the overarching theme for each. Compare and contrast the use of revolution and power in different genres.

— Visit a sixth-grade class so that students may share their books with younger students. Conduct a literary critique with the class regarding the books. You may want to use the Newbery/Caldecott criteria as a reference for the critique.

◆ Extensions
—Independent Research

1. Research what happened to the loyalists following the American Revolution. Become a loyalist. Write a diary detailing what you were enduring during the final weeks of the war, what you felt, how you were treated, and what happened once the war was ended. Make the diary appear to be authentic (old and worn looking). Share it with your classmates.

2. The power of war often brings with it abuse and atrocities. Research the treatment of the American soldiers who were kept aboard prison ships in the Brooklyn Harbor in which 11,500 Americans died. Construct a model of the ship. Describe what happened to the ships following the war.

3. In 1804, Ludwig Van Beethoven composed his Third Symphony, *Eroica* ("Heroic"), and dedicated it to one of the world's most powerful men, Napoleon. Find other pieces of music that were either written or dedicated to powerful leaders. Have a "Concert of Power" with the selections of music being played (from a recording) or performed for the audience. Give a brief explanation of each musical piece before it is shared with the audience.

4. Create a card fact file that describes pieces of art from a time of "Artistic Revolution." The revolution should include art from impressionism to realism, romanticism, modernism, and generated from a computer.

5. Many people forget the heroic actions of Benedict Arnold and the important contributions he made to the patriots during the beginning of the war. Research both his positive and negative contributions to the efforts of the revolution. Stage a mock trial of Benedict Arnold with several of your classmates.

6. Find out about the Committee for Public Safety during the French Revolution. What was its function? Did it help to ensure the safety of the citizens of France? Write an editorial about your view regarding the committee. Create a cartoon to accompany your editorial.

7. Read some of the writings of Thomas Paine, such as his pamphlet *Common Sense*. Study the way he used the English language and the clear simplicity of his thoughts. Think of an ethical issue today in the U.S. in which you feel people should become involved in order to create a change. Design a pamphlet espousing your point of view. Make sure that the message is delivered in a clear, easy-to-read manner.

8. Create floor maps of a major battle or incident from one of the two revolutions. Research the battle and create a map on a three-square-foot piece of muslin. The map may be painted or colored with markers. Create flags or some other type of movable object in order to show the movement of opposing forces on the map. Enact the battle with classmates.

—Classical Connections: Philosophy

Georg Hegel, the German philosopher, developed the idea of the *dialectic*, in which every idea (*thesis*) is contradicted by another idea (*antithesis*), and the conflict between the two produces an agreement (*synthesis*). Select a revolution and identify the *thesis* factors, the *antithesis* responses, and the *synthesis* compromises that resulted. Present the dialectic in the form of posters or other visual media.

—Literary Connections

1. To really appreciate the power of reading, find a copy of the ballad "Learning to Read" by Frances Harper. The ballad takes place during Reconstruction. Aunt Chloe, an ex-slave, longs to read. When she's over 60 years old, she teaches herself to read the Testaments and Hymns. Perform the ballad for your classmates.
2. For a sense of France during the time of the Revolution, read either *A Tale of Two Cities* or *The Scarlet Pimpernel*. Both have been made into movies. Compare and contrast the movie version to the books.

—Adaptations for Other Grade Levels

1. Limit the study of revolution and power to the American Revolution.
2. Students may create books depicting causes of the revolution or major battles.

Study Starter: Conflict Chart

Conflict	Causes	Prominent Figures	Major Incidents	Resolution	Was conflict justified? Explain.
American Revolution Date: Parties involved in the conflict:	Economic: Political: Social:				
French Revolution Date: Parties involved in the conflict:	Economic: Political: Social:				

Revolutions in Art

Revolutions in art can be as fascinating and disturbing as political upheavals.

The word *dada* is the French word for "hobby horse." Dadasim, however, refers to an art movement in Europe that lasted six years (1916–1922). The French artist, Marcel Duchamp, and some of his contemporaries randomly picked a word from a dictionary to represent this art movement. The word dada, with its infantile sound, worked well as an "all-purpose word." The purpose of Dadaism was to bring attention to the meaningless losses incurred by the catastrophes of World War I. The issues of morality and aesthetics were of no consequence in the context of war and its nihilism and indifference to humanity. Duchamp insulted everything that was normal and every cliché about art. Dadaism was a reflection of the disillusionment brought on by the war. The artists questioned the value of the development of science and technology for bringing Europe to the brink of destruction. Consequently the artists produced art that reflected the absurdity of the world that was falling apart around them.

Dada was antiart, a philosophical movement that questioned everything about art and that alone created an attitude that encouraged rethinking of the conceptualization of art. It was critical of conventional techniques and of the materials used to make art. Marcel Duchamp created a series of sculptures he appropriately called "Ready-Mades," items that suggested that anything could be considered art if the artist chose to call it art. A common object would lose its original function and acquire an aesthetic worth. One example of this shift of function was his showing of a bottle rack in Paris in 1913. Placed inside a gallery, the ordinary European bottle rack became a sculpture.

Objective

The students will find examples of revolutions in the 20th century and create art objects that will bring attention to the issues.

Materials

- published materials regarding issues dealing with revolutions in the 20th century
- newsprint drawing paper
- ruled paper
- pencils
- erasers
- found objects (must be approved by the teacher)
- art materials

Procedure

1. The students will select their topics and then brainstorm their ideas for artwork that will bring attention to the issues surrounding their topics.
2. The students will sketch their ideas on the newsprint. Sketches must be submitted for both one-dimensional and two-dimensional concepts.
3. Upon approval from the teacher, the students will gather the materials needed to create the artwork.

4. Artwork will be presented to the class. Student will explain the artwork that was created.

Evaluation

Did the student produce an artwork that was well designed? Did the art work visually bring attention to the issues of the revolution?

Art Reference Books

The art book (1998). London: Phaidon.

Janson, H. W. (1997). *The history of art.* New York: H. Abrams.

Strickland, C. & Boswell, J. (1992). *The annotated Mona Lisa: A crash course in art history from prehistoric to postmodern.* Kansas City: Andrews & McNeel.

Tansey, R. (1995). *Gardner's art through the ages.* New York: HBJ.

Probability & Statistics:
Making Decisions

I. Teacher Preparation

◆ **Background**
Time Required: 6–8 class periods

Getting Ready
For this lesson you will need the following:
- Internet access; and
- art materials.

Curriculum Standards

The student will:

Primary Standard
- Evaluate predictions and conclusions based on statistical data.

Embedded Content and Skills
- Apply appropriate mathematical skills to solve problems connected to everyday experiences, investigations in other disciplines, and activities in and outside of school.
- Understand that different forms of numbers are appropriate for different situations.
- Use statistical procedures to describe data.

Curriculum Standard Level:
Introductory   **Developmental X**   Extension

◆ Framework

Theme: Power

Generalization: Power is the ability to influence. Power may be used for "good" or abused. Power may be used to facilitate, dominate, or maintain the status quo.

Content Focus: Probability and Statistics—the students will look at the ethical issues regarding the use and interpretation of statistical data, methods of surveying and sampling, and the power of data to influence and describe.

Rationale: The study of probability and statistics gives students insight into how different disciplines use data.

Differentiation Framework

Thinking Skills	Depth/Complexity	Research	Products
• Compare and contrast • Identify attributes • Recognize relationships • State assumptions • Judge with criteria	• Details • Patterns • Rules • Trends • Ethics • Different perspectives	• Internet resources • Media resources • Reference books • Interviews	• Debate • Survey and graph results • Charts • Photo essay

Thinking Skills

- **Compare and contrast**—note similarities and differences.
  Example: Students will compare and contrast methods of surveying and sampling data.
- **Identify attributes**—describe qualities and characteristics.
  Example: Students will identify the characteristics of ethical sampling and surveying.
- **Recognize relationships**—understanding connections among different entities.
  Example: Students will relate purpose and truth in using statistical data.
- **State assumptions**—explaining underlying concepts.
  Example: Students will demonstrate how to state and prove assumptions.
- **Judge with criteria**—make decisions based on standards.
  Example: Students will establish criteria to judge the efficacy of a survey.

Depth/Complexity

- **Details**—parts, attributes, factors, and variables.
  Example: Students will identify details of a good survey.
- **Patterns**—repetition; predictability.
  Example: Students will note recurring patterns and trends in the predicting and presenting of statistical information.

- **Rules**—structure, order, hierarchy.
  Example: Students will identify rules for surveying.
- **Trends**—influences; course of direction.
  Example: Students will demonstrate how trends are reflected in surveys.
- **Ethics**—different opinions; point of view; judgment.
  Example: Students will define where and how ethics are reflected in surveys.
- **Different perspectives**—multiple perspectives; opposing viewpoints; differing roles and knowledge.
  Example: Students will use different points of view to solve problems in the simulation.

Research

Students will use a variety of reference resources including the Internet, media resources, books, and interviews to gather data for decision making.

Product

Students will present results in the form of charts, picture/photo essays, and/or debates based on controversial issues.

II. The Lesson

◆ Motivation

- Discuss with students the purpose and value of studying statistics in mathematics. (see Teacher Notes below for an interesting slant). Generate other examples of the value of statistics as a study. Conduct a survey in the school or local mall to validate the importance of statistics in daily life.

◆ Input

1. Elicit examples of where and when simulations are used, including job training and games.
2. Introduce students to the elements that define the simulation they will be playing (see "Simulation: Team Decision" Study Starter).

Teacher Notes

The Case of the Chocolate Chip Cookies. A well-known cookie company stated in advertisements that they had 1,000 chips per bag of chocolate chip cookies. Students in a science lab investigated (counted the chips!) and determined that this was false advertising, because indeed they did not have 1,000 chips in the bag. The company had to add more chips.

3. Explain the purpose of a simulation as a method of experiencing some things in the real world. Explain that a simulation has these features: scenario or setting, roles to enact, and problem(s) to solve.
4. Divide the class into groups to play and assign the roles for members in each group.
5. Define the problem and the directions for the simulation (see Teacher Notes on p. 154 for suggested sources of information). Allow students time to research and gather data to support their assigned role (use "Scenario Worksheet" Study Starter).

Our Solutions	Statistical Evidence
• Group 1	
• Group 2	
• Group 3	

6. During the simulation research, stop the simulation and ask the students: 1) What have you accomplished so far? 2) What needs do you have?

7. Introduce a new variable to the students at this time. For example, the deadline for new business for the nation's meeting is in one hour. All committees must be ready to present their solution.

8. Share the solutions to the problem and complete the retrieval chart.

9. Use the chart to assess the solutions to the problem based in the simulation by asking these questions: 1) What evidence can be used to judge these solutions? 2) Which solutions appear to require the most preparation in order to be implemented?

10. Ask why and how simulations and their solutions can be applied to real life. *(Note: This step is the most important.)* Which solution do think will be most probable for the United States to implement?

◆ **Output**

1. Have students develop a list of controversial issues of interest to themselves, their school, and/or community. Students (in groups) select one issue for research. Develop a survey with four or five statements about your topic. Statements ("The city needs a curfew for teenagers") should be followed by a scale for recording responses.

Teacher Notes

See the following sites for information:

- http://www.gunfree.org—The Coalition to Stop Gun Violence (CSGV) was founded in 1974 to combat the growing gun violence problem in the United States.
- http://www.handguncontrol.org—Hand Control Incorporated works to enact stronger federal, state, and local gun control laws, but does not seek to ban handguns.
- http://www.vpc.org/ytopic—Violence Policy Center links to documents relating guns and youth violence.
- http://www.waceasefire.org—Information about the organization and a compilation of the latest gun violence-related news from around the country.
- http://rkba.org—Firearms and firearms rights links.
- http://www.abcnews.go.com/sections/us/Daily News/guns_poll990518.html—Support for Gun Control Stable.
- http://www.potomac-inc.org/index.html—The Firearms Policy Journal has been discontinued and reinvented (Oct. 1998) as the Potomac Institute, a 501(c)(3) nonprofit corporation.

	strongly agree	agree	undecided	disagree	strongly disagree
The city needs a curfew for teenagers.	_____	_____	_____	_____	_____

2. Give the survey to as many people as possible. Get responses from males and females, as well as individuals of different age groups and backgrounds.
3. Total the responses, find percentages, and graph the results for each question. Share responses with the class.
4. Discuss the following questions:
    - How would the results have been different if you had asked only males? Females? Students? Parents?
    - How might your results be different if you had asked less than 10 people?
    - What other factors might influence your results?

◆ Culmination

1. Present the definition of *ethics*: "Ethics in philosophy, the study and evaluation of human conduct in the light of moral principles, which may be viewed as the individual's standard of conduct or as a body of social obligations and duties." [Reference: Ask Jeeves! Presents Encyclopedia.com, http://aj.encyclopedia.com]
2. Describe and discuss the types and importance of ethics in different contexts.
3. Recognize the implications of ethics in these categories: academic, social, political, and personal.
4. Describe the rules and patterns of ethics in each category.
5. Discuss what types of ethics were involved in the simulation.
6. Present the statement: Power may be used to facilitate, dominate, or maintain the status quo.
7. Relate this generalization to the study or application of ethics.

◆ Extensions

—Independent Research Topics

1. Explore the ethics involved in surveying, sampling, and reporting data.
    - Investigate the methods of surveying and sampling to gather data.
    - Research and generate graphs that share the results of your study.
    - Dramatize your findings as a statistician by making charts and develop a photo essay in the manner of a statistician's report.
    - State an assumption related to the theme of power when creating your presentation.
2. Other presentation options:
    - Write a talk radio show discussing your findings.
    - Write a news article about your findings.

—Interdisciplinary options

- Select a controversial issue (political, social, scientific, artistic) from current events, history, or literature and develop a scenario using the one from the lesson as a model. Develop a statement that can be approached from more than one perspective. ("Social Security must be saved at all costs." "The U.S. has a duty to intervene in foreign politics.") Create a list of participants that reflects diverse points of view on the issue. Use the "Scenario Worksheet" Study Starter to record results. Debate or discuss the issue and reach a consensus.

—Adaptations for Other Grade Levels
1. Grades 5 and under: Shorten the lesson by eliminating the Culmination activity.
2. Grade 9: Apply the categories of ethics to another area of study in mathematics.

Simulation:
Team Decision

Scenario

The nation you live in is beginning to have problems with guns. The guns are being used in improper ways and people are being injured and killed. Citizens are divided as to how to address this situation.

Roles

The role of each member of the team is to collect statistical data that best represents his or her assigned point of view and present the data to the team.

1. **National Rifle Association representative:** You believe that people have a Constitutional right to own guns.
2. **Teacher:** You are to present an objective opinion, favoring neither side.
3. **Parent:** You are a parent of three small children and worry about the life that lies ahead for them. You want them to grow up in a safe world.
4. **Family member of someone killed by gun violence:** You have just lost a family member to gun violence. Before the killing, you were pro-gun; now you are anti-gun.
5. **Teen #1:** You are a teenager from a small town. You want to have the right to carry a gun.
6. **Teen #2:** You are a teenager in a large city in the nation. You are against private ownership of guns.
7. **Government official:** Your job is to protect the citizens of the nation. You are only interested in what is Constitutionally correct.
8. **Gun manufacturer:** Your company makes many kinds of guns and employs hundreds of people.
9. **Reporter:** You are reporting on this issue for a major news magazine.

Problem to Solve

As members of the team chosen to make a decision on what to do about the gun problem, research the issue and come to a consensus. Determine what plan your team will propose to the representatives of your nation.

Simulation:
Scenario Worksheet

Role assigned: _____

Problem as you see it from the perspective of the role:_____

_____

_____

Key points to research: _____

_____

_____

Solutions to suggest to council: _____

_____

_____

Final group decision: _____

_____

_____

When Is it Art?

Making decisions in art requires thought, planning, and execution.

Art as we know it has evolved from the cave paintings of prehistoric humans, to Grecian architecture, to the *Mona Lisa*, to Van Gogh's *Starry Night*, to the murals of Rivera, Siqueiros, and Orozco, to Picasso's cubist paintings, to Magritte's surrealism and Pollock's action paintings, to Christo's *Running Fence*, and to Keith Haring's icons in the subways of New York City. It has challenged our perceptions of what art is. In the last half of the 20th century alone, the art world witnessed over 60 different art movements.

Of course, the audience was not made up entirely of artists and patrons of the arts. Often, the average person not educated in the arts became the audience for creative works that were sometimes shocking and completely detached from preconceived notions of what art is or should be. At the earliest level of art appreciation, people tend to rate artwork according to the skill demonstrated in the artist's ability to imitate reality. The aesthetic theory of **Imitationalism** focuses on imitating reality through visual representation. The earliest works of art were following this aesthetic theory because the artists were producing images that were recognizable to people. We are usually impressed by the child who demonstrates the ability to draw something realistically; however, art is more than a vehicle to imitate life.

Artists are also concerned with the aesthetic theory of **Emotionalism**. This is evident in works that arouse an instant emotional reaction from the viewer. *The Third of May, 1808* by Francisco Goya is one such work. Before you notice the skill with which Goya painted this dramatic scene, your emotions react to the moment that he has captured on canvas. Your criticism of his artwork can be based on the theories both of Emotionalism and Imitationalism. You can also appreciate the artwork for its application of the theory of **Formalism**. This theory regards the artist's use of the elements and principles of art: How did the artist use color, value, texture, space, shape, line, and form? How did the artist apply proportion, pattern, movement, rhythm, unity, emphasis, and balance? Some works of art make no visual references to Emotionalism or Imitationalism. Donald Judd's untitled stainless steel boxes are only about form and eliminate the artist's involvement in the production of the sculptures. The pieces were manufactured by a company, not by the artist who designed them. Judd was a minimalist, an artist who designed sculptures of basic geometric form. His work focused on the theory of Formalism.

It is important that we understand the aesthetic theories because they enable us to appreciate works of art, especially those with which we are unfamiliar. When is something art? First, it should be a work that has been created by someone. It should have evolved from a concept that was imagined or conceived by someone. It is the end result of someone's effort to communicate a thought. It can be approached through Imitationalism, Emotionalism, Formalism, or combinations of the three.

Objective

Each student will create a unique work of art that clearly represents one of the theories of art. The theories are Imitationalism, Emotionalism, and Formalism.

Materials

art history books
pencils
paper
found materials
cardboard
poster board
white glue
scissors
markers
tempera paints
watercolors
brushes
pastels
crayons
chalk

Procedure

1. Select a theory of art on which to focus. Each student will write down the theory he or she has chosen to use on a sheet of paper that he or she will turn in to the teacher. Students must not discuss their selection with anyone.
2. The teacher will determine how much time they have to work on their artwork. The artwork may be two-dimensional or three-dimensional.
3. After completing their compositions, the students will display them in the classroom. The teacher will ask students which theories apply to the objects.
4. This should be a process of discovery. The students should cooperate in a respectful manner. The students should focus on the dominant aesthetic feature of the work of art. Remember Goya's *The Third of May, 1808.*

Evaluation

Did the students recognize the aesthetic theories that were used? Were the students creative?

Art Reference Books

The art book. (1998). London: Phaidon.

Janson, H. W. (1997). *The history of art.* New York: H. Abrams.

Strickland, C. & Boswell, J. (1992). *The annotated Mona Lisa: A crash course in crt history from prehistoric to postmodern.* Kansas City: Andrews & McNeel.

Tansey, R. (1995). *Gardner's art through the ages.* New York: HBJ.

Ideas Behind the Art: Aesthetic Theories

When is something art? First, it should be a work that has been created by someone. It should have evolved from a concept that was imagined or conceived by someone. It is the end result of someone's effort to communicate a thought.

Imitationalism—Looks at how well works imitate reality through visual representation. How realistic is the representation?

Emotionalism—Examines works that arouse an instant emotional reaction from the viewer. How well does the artist engage our emotional interest?

Formalism—Regards the artists' use of the elements and principles of art. How did the artist use color, value, texture, space, shape, line and form? How did the artist apply proportion, pattern, movement, rhythm, unity, emphasis, and balance?

- Select a theory of art and write it down on a sheet of paper. Turn this in to the teacher, but do not discuss the choice with anyone.

- Using the principles of the selected theory, create a unique work of art that clearly represents one of these theories.

Extinction

I. Teacher Preparation

◆ **Background**
Time Required: 5–10 class periods

Getting Ready
For this lesson you will need the following:
- *Baaa*, by David Macaulay;
- *The Story of Rosy Dock*, by Jeannie Baker;
- *And Then There Was One*, by Margery Flacklam and Pamela Johnson; and
- lists of endangered animals.

Curriculum Standards

The student will:

Primary Standard
- Understand that natural events and human activities can alter the equilibrium of natural and designed systems.

Embedded Content and Skills
- Explain the interdependence among living systems.

Curriculum Standard Level:
Introductory   Developmental   **Extension X**

◆ Framework

Theme: Power

Generalization: The use of power has advantages and disadvantages for the survival of individual species.

Content Focus: Extinction—the dying out of a species of plant or animal. Natural and human events contribute to extinction.

Rationale: In order to approach the concept of extinction, students need to understand the impact of both natural and human power on the process of change in nature.

Differentiation Framework

Thinking Skills	Depth/Complexity	Research	Products
• Categorize • Note ambiguity • Identify attributes • Summarize	• Language of discipline • Details • Patterns • Change over time • Ethics	• Internet resources • Reference materials	• Chart research results

Thinking Skills

- **Categorize**—placing individuals or concepts in specific classifications.
  Example: Students will classify use of power over time.
- **Note ambiguity**—become aware of uncertainty and multiple meanings.
  Example: Students will list controversial issues in the readings.
- **Identify attributes**—note identifying characteristics.
  Example: Students will note ethical questions of the use of power.
- **Summarize**—present the general idea in a brief form.
  Example: Students will make generalizations about the use of power and its impact on nature.

Depth/Complexity

- **Language of the discipline**—specialized vocabulary, tools used by the discipline.
  Example: Students will use language appropriate to science in writing.
- **Details**—basic facts, ideas, and concepts of the discipline.
  Example: Students will use facts and details to make judgments.
- **Patterns**—repetition; predictability.
  Example: Students will list patterns of the use of power.
- **Change over time**—relationships over past, present, and future.
  Example: Students will chart changes in ethical treatment of animals.

• **Ethics**—different opinions; judging.
Example: Students will consider the ideas of power in relation to endangered species.

Research

• **Internet resources**—use search engines to locate Web sites with useful information.
Example: Students will retrieve information about endangered animals from a variety of Web sites.

• **Reference materials**—a variety of text and media information.
Example: Students will use a number of reference sources to gather information on endangered species and animal extinction

Product

Students will chart the influence of the use of power on endangered animals.

II. The Lesson

◆ **Motivation**

Read *Baaa* by David Macaulay in a large group or have students read the text in small discussion groups. This may be assigned several days in advance.

◆ **Input**

1. Have students summarize the story and use the following questions to prompt discussion about power.
   • What examples of power did you find in the book?
   • What issues in the book are controversial?
   • Does the book contain any ethical considerations?
2. Record student responses on a chart.
3. Ask the students what unanswered questions they have about power after reading the book. Have the students record their questions on a chart.

Teacher Notes

Endangered species—a species that is threatened with extinction.

Internet Resources:
• http://www.worldkids.net/eac/fastfact.htm—Fast facts about endangered species.
• http://www.wcmc.org.uk/cgi-bin/arl_input.p—World Conservation Monitoring Center.
• http://www.tmmc.org/endanger.htm—Endangered marine animals.

Other Resource Materials:
• lists of endangered animals
• addresses of animal protection agencies

Examples of Power	Controversial Issues	Ethical Considerations

◆ Output

1. Distribute the unanswered questions to small groups or individuals to focus their research.

2. Challenge them to find the answers to the questions by studying patterns of power over time and ethics of power over time related to issues or events that have contributed to the extinction of a species. Distribute copies of the "Extinction: Power and Ethics" Study Starter to each research group to record findings.

◆ Culmination

1. Have each individual or group present their findings to the class in chart form. Ask the students what evidence they found that shows how patterns of power and ethics of power change over time and how these affect the extinction of animal species. Post the charts or prepare overhead transparencies of the research results.

2. Analyze the charts by categorizing the patterns and ethics of power over time into advantages and disadvantages. Mark the advantages (humanity's positive relationship with nature) with one color and the disadvantages with another color.

3. Summarize by challenging the students to use evidence from their research to prove the generalization that the use of power has advantages and disadvantages.

Question(s)	Patterns of Power	Ethics of Power

◆ Extensions

—Independent Research Topics

1. Choose an endangered species and chart the examples of power contributing to extinction. Note what measures can be taken to turn power into an advantage and how natural and human events can contribute to the preservation of the endangered species.

2. Choose an endangered species and initiate an active campaign to protect it.

3. Investigate the particular genetic traits of an endangered or extinct species. Identify traits that may be a factor in the endangered/extinct status of the species. Locate other species with similar traits and report on how these species might be protected. Present findings in an illustrated poster display or essay.

—Interdisciplinary options

1. Begin a letter writing campaign.

2. Lobby before a local or state committee.

3. Create brochures and posters and send them to an established agency, interested committee, or lobbyist.

Extinction:
Power and Ethics

After reading David Macauley's *Baaa*, list your unanswered questions in the first column. Research the questions and record your findings about the use of power and ethical considerations for endangered animals in the other columns.

Unanswered Questions	Patterns of Power Over Time	Ethics of Power Over Time

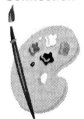

Art in Our LIves

Changes in civilization affect art, as well as nature. The illuminated manuscript, like an endangered plant or animal, almost disappeared in the face of cultural changes.

Artists throughout history have been faced with changes due to the evolution of science and technology. Some of the changes have helped to advance creative processes. For example, the invention of oil paints in tubes along with the use of new synthetic pigments shortened the preparatory time for painting with oil paints. Prior to using paints from tubes, artists had to mix their own paints by combining pulverized pigments with linseed oil. This was a time-consuming and arduous process. One artist who was especially pleased with the new convenience was Vincent van Gogh. In letters he wrote to his brother Theo, who sent him money and supplies for painting, van Gogh expressed his delight with oil paints from tubes. On occasion, he even painted directly on the canvas with the tubes of brilliant colors. The Aborigines of Australia have also embraced modern products. They use acrylic paints to continue traditions of image making that date back to the times of cave and rock paintings. Today their contemporary versions of ancient iconography are sold in art galleries throughout Australia.

In the 15th century, the invention of the printing press and the growing popularity of paper in Europe ended an artful era of bookmaking. Dating as far back as the early fifth century A.D., manuscripts were written and illustrated on either vellum or parchment—thin, bleached animal hide from lambs, goats, and calves. Artists were commissioned to illustrate the manuscripts with illuminations—miniature tempera paintings that were usually gilded with gold. The process would take up to three years to complete. The illuminations were masterfully painted in books that could be as small as the size of a hand or as large as 18" x 24". Printing proved to be a major advancement for illustration, as well as the written word. Printing woodcut images replaced the time-consuming processes involved in illuminations. The printed illustrations were simple linear designs, lacking the intricacies of color, depth, and skillfully rendered detail. Nevertheless, woodcuts, which could make thousands of prints from one block, became the standard for printed texts. The illuminated manuscript became obsolete.

Objective
The students will create compositions that illuminate their names.

Materials
- newsprint paper
- parchment paper
- pencils (colored and regular)
- erasers
- rulers
- fine-point felt-tipped pens

Procedure

1. Cut the parchment paper and newsprint paper in half. The dimensions should be 4¼" x 11". Preliminary sketching will be drawn on the newsprint.

2. The students will choose to illuminate either their first or last name. A deciding factor might be the first letter of the name. The illumination of the name will begin with the design of a decorative letter for the first letter of the name.

3. Draw a two-inch square. The decorative letter will occupy the space within the square. The letter should compliment the style of lettering that the student selects, as well as the scene that illuminates the name. Decorative letters are a part of the theme of the illumination.

4. Draw a straight horizontal line next to the decorative letter square. The remaining letters of the name should be spaced on this line. A second line might be necessary to establish the height of the letters.

5. Once the lettering is complete, the students will trace the name onto the parchment paper. Simply place the parchment paper over the newsprint paper and trace.

6. Draw lightly. After the name is traced, draw the illumination on the parchment paper.

7. Next, add color with the colored pencils.

8. Trace the outline of the decorative letter and other letters with the fine-point felt-tipped pen.

Evaluation

Did the student create a colorful illumination using creative lettering? Did the illumination and the lettering adhere to a common theme?

Art Reference Books

The art book (1998). London: Phaidon.

Janson, H. W. (1997). *The history of art.* New York: H. Abrams.

Strickland, C. & Boswell, J. (1992). *The annotated Mona Lisa: A crash course in art history from prehistoric to postmodern.* Kansas City: Andrews & McNeel.

Tansey, R. (1995). *Gardner's art through the ages.* New York: HBJ.

Curriculum Standards Correlations With Texas Essential Knowledge and Skills (TEKS)

For teachers in Texas, following are listed the TEKS correlations for each lesson.

Grade 6

- **Language Arts**

  The student will:

  — **Recognize the distinguishing features of genre. (6.12)**
  — Use effective rate, volume, pitch, and tone for the audience and setting. (6.5E)
  — Read for varied purposes such as to be informed, to be entertained, to appreciate the writer's craft, and to discover models for his or her own writing. (6.8C)
  — Interpret text ideas through such varied means as journal writing discussion, enactment, and media. (6.11B)
  — Connect, compare, and contrast ideas, themes, and issues across a text. (6.11D)
  — Capitalize and punctuate correctly to clarify and enhance meaning such as capitalizing titles, using hyphens, semicolons, colons, possessives, and sentence punctuation. (6.16B)

- **Social Studies**

  The student will:

  — **Explain the relationship among religious ideas, philosophical ideas, and cultures. (6.19A)**
  — Describe characteristics of selected contemporary societies that resulted from historical events and analyze background of societies that resulted from historical events. (6.1A, B)
  — Explain the significance of individuals from selected societies past and present and their influence on selected historical and contemporary societies. (6.2 A, B)
  — Explain how opportunities for citizens to participate in and influence the political process vary among selected contemporary societies. (6.13B)
  — Analyze similarities and differences among selected world societies and explain examples of conflict between and among cultures. (6.15 C, D)
  — Compare characteristics of institutions in selected contemporary societies. (6.16 B)
  — Explain aspects that link or separate cultures and societies. (6.17 A–CD)

- **Mathematics**

  The student will:

  — **Use statistical representations to analyze data. (6.10)**
  — Apply grade-6 mathematics to solve problems connected to everyday experiences, investigations in other disciplines, and activities in and outside of school. (6.11)

- **Science**

  The student will:

  — **Know that the traits of a species can change through generations and that the instructions for traits are contained in the genetic material of the organisms. (6.11)**

  — Conduct field and laboratory investigations using safe, environmentally appropriate, and ethical practices. (6.1)

  — Use scientific inquiry methods during field and laboratory investigations. (6.2)

  — Use critical thinking and scientific problem solving to make informed decisions. (6.3)

  — Use a variety of tools and methods to conduct science inquiry. (6.4)

Grade 7

- **Language Arts**

  The student will:

  — **Recognize the distinguishing features of genres. (7.12 B)**

  — Read classic and contemporary works. (7.8A)

  — Find similarities and differences such as in treatment, scope, or organization. (7.10 I)

  — Analyze characters traits, motivations, conflicts, point of view, relationships, and changes they undergo. (7.12 F)

  — Collaborate with other writers to compose, organize, and revise. (7.21 A)

  — Use effective rate, volume, pitch, and tone for the audience and setting. (7.5 E)

- **Social Studies**

  The student will:

  — **Explain how the diversity of Texas is reflected in a variety of cultural activities, celebrations, and performances. 7.19 A**

  — Pose and answer questions about geographic distributions and patterns. (7.8 B)

  — Trace the development of major industries. (7.12 B)

  — Describe the importance of free speech and press and defend a point of view on Texas. (7.17 B,C)

  — Evaluate the effects of scientific discoveries in Texas. (7.20 D)

- **Mathematics**

  The student will:

  — **Understand that the way a set of data is displayed influences its interpretation. (7.11)**

  — Use measures of central tendency and range to describe a set of data. (7.12)

  — Select and use an appropriate representation for presenting collected data and justify the selection. (7.11 A)

  — Describe a set of data using mean, median, mode, and range. (7.12 A)

  — Determine solution strategies and will analyze or solve problems. (7.12 B)

  — Make inferences and convincing arguments based on an analysis of given or collected data. (7.11 B)

- **Science**

  The student will:

  — **Investigate the relationship between organisms and the environment. (7.12)**

— Chart the relationship between structure and function in living systems. (7.9)

— Interpret the responses of organisms caused by internal or external stimuli. (7.11)

— Analyze the relationship between organisms and the environment. (7.12)

— Explain how natural events and human activity can alter Earth systems. (7.14)

Grade 8

- **Language Arts**

The student will:

— **Recognize the distinguishing features of genres including historical fiction. (8.12 B)**

— Draw inferences or generalizations and support them with text evidence. (8.10 H)

— Interpret text ideas through such varied means as journal writing and discussion. (8.11 B)

— Analyze characters, traits, motivations, conflicts, points of view, relationships, and changes they undergo. (8.12 F)

— Produce written texts by organizing ideas, using effective transitions, and choosing precise working. (8.15 H)

- **Social Studies**

The student will:

— **Analyze causes of the American Revolution, including mercantilism and British economic policies following the French and Indian War. (8.4 A; 8.24 C)**

— Understand traditional historical points of reference in U.S. history. (8.1)

— List the foundations of representative government in the United States. (8.3)

— Explain the locations and characteristics of places and regions of the United States, past and present. (8.11)

— Understand the origins and development of the free enterprise system in the United States. (8.15)

— Explain important American beliefs reflected in the U.S. Constitution and other documents. (8.16)

— Understand the importance of accepting personal responsibility. (8.20 C)

— Explain the contributions of the Founding Fathers as models of civic virtue. (8.21 B)

- **Mathematics**

The student will:

— **Evaluate predictions and conclusions based on statistical data. (8.13)**

— Apply grade-8 mathematics to solve problems connected to everyday experiences, investigations in other disciplines, and activities in and outside of school. (8.14)

— Understand that different forms of numbers are appropriate for different situations. (8.1)

— Use statistical procedures to describe data.(8.12)

- **Science**

The student will:

— **Understand that natural events and human activities can alter Earth systems. (8.14)**

— Explain the interdependence among living systems. (8.6)

ACTIVITIES FOR ADVANCED LEARNING SERIES

Camp Fraction
Solving Exciting Word Problems Using Fractions
Set around a trip to summer camp, students work with fractions in a problem-solving format, while learning a little history, trivia, and fun facts about a number of different items.
Grades 4–6 $11.95

Creative Writing
Using Fairy Tales to Enrich Writing Skills
Use fairy tales to challenge and motivate your students. This activity book contains fun reading and writing activities that pique students' interest in creative writing.
Grades 4–8 $11.95

Extra! Extra!
Advanced Reading and Writing Activities for Language Arts
The book includes standards-based independent language arts activities for students in grades K–2 such as developing a newspaper and inventing new words.
Grades K-2 $11.95

Math Problem Solvers
Using Word Problems to Enhance Mathematical Problem Solving Skills
The standards-based problem solving strategies addressed in this book include drawing a picture, looking for a pattern, guessing and checking, acting it out, making a table or list, and working backwards.
Grades 2–3 $11.95

Puzzled by Math!
Using Puzzles to Teach Math Skills
Puzzled by Math! offers a collection of mathematical equations, knowledge, and skills in puzzle form. Standards-based content addresses addition, subtraction, multiplication, division, fractions, decimals, and algebra. Thirty-five exciting and challenging puzzles are included, as well as suggestions for using the material for a classroom learning center.
Grades 3–7 $11.95

Survival on the Reef
Exploring Amazing Animals and the Ways They Adapt to Their Environment
This challenging activity book addresses many essential skills and knowledge contained in the National Science Teachers Association standards using activities focused on the exciting environment of a coral reef, its inhabitants, and the ways these inhabitants have adapted to their world.
Grades 2–3 $11.95

Writing Stretchers
15 Minute Activities to Enrich Writing Skills
Standards-based activities address the areas of reading, writing, vocabulary, content literacy, creativity, and thinking skills, giving students a chance to enrich their writing skills.
Grades 4–8 $11.95

For a complete listing of titles in this series, please visit our website at

http://www.prufrock.com

PRUFROCK PRESS INC.